★ ★ ★ KID ★ ★ ★
OLYMPIANS
SUMMER

TRUE TALES OF CHILDHOOD FROM CHAMPIONS AND GAME CHANGERS

STORIES BY *ROBIN STEVENSON*   ILLUSTRATIONS BY *ALLISON STEINFELD*

MEGAN RAPINOE

SERENA WILLIAMS

SIMONE BILES

MICHAEL PHELPS

KID OLYMPIANS

SUMMER

TRUE TALES OF CHILDHOOD FROM CHAMPIONS AND GAME CHANGERS

STORIES BY *ROBIN STEVENSON* ILLUSTRATIONS BY *ALLISON STEINFELD*

DICK FOSBURY

USAIN BOLT

IBTIHAJ MUHAMMAD

TATYANA MCFADDEN

Library of Congress Cataloging-in-Publication Data
Names: Stevenson, Robin, 1968- author. | Steinfeld, Allison, illustrator.
Title: Kid Olympians, summer : true tales of childhood from champions and game changers / stories by Robin Stevenson ; illustrations by Allison Steinfeld.
Description: Philadelphia : Quirk Books, 2024. | Series: Kid legends | Includes bibliographical references and index. | Audience: Ages 9-12 | Summary: "Childhood biographies of sixteen athletes who have competed in the Summer Olympic and Paralympic Games"— Provided by publisher.
Identifiers: LCCN 2023022089 (print) | LCCN 2023022090 (ebook) | ISBN 9781683693710 (hardcover) | ISBN 9781683693727 (ebook)
Subjects: LCSH: Olympic athletes—Biography—Juvenile literature. | Child athletes—Biography—Juvenile literature.
Classification: LCC GV721.53 .S74 2024 (print) | LCC GV721.53 (ebook) | DDC 796.092/2—dc23/eng/20230602
LC record available at https://lccn.loc.gov/2023022089
LC ebook record available at https://lccn.loc.gov/2023022090

ISBN: 978-1-68369-371-0

Printed in China

Typeset in Bulmer MT, Bell MT, Linowrite, and Bulldog

Designed by Elissa Flanigan
Illustrations by Allison Steinfeld
Production management by John J. McGurk

Quirk Books
215 Church Street
Philadelphia, PA 19106
quirkbooks.com

10 9 8 7 6 5 4 3 2 1

To Milo, Riley, Evan, and Atalia

Table of Contents

PART 3

Swimming into Summer

PART 4

Speaking Out

Introduction

You've probably watched the Summer Olympics and Paralympics on television: Runners and wheelchair racers, tearing down the track at lightning speed. Gymnasts, all power and grace as they spin around the bars and flip across the floor. Swimmers, swiftly powering through the water, as smoothly as fish.

For many young athletes around the world, competing at the Olympics is the ultimate dream. But long before they made it to international competitions, all the Olympians in this book were little kids who liked to run, jump, and play . . . a lot!

Gymnast Nadia Comăneci liked jumping on beds and climbing trees—including, on one occasion, the Christmas tree in her living room. From the time she could speak, swimmer Ellie Simmonds constantly asked her mom what they would be doing that day—she needed to be busy and active. And many years before he became the world's fastest sprinter, Usain Bolt was exhausting his parents by running everywhere and climbing everything.

Some of these Olympians had parents who helped them get involved in sports at a very young age. Nadia Comăneci's mother signed her up for gymnastics at five, to give her an outlet for her endless energy. Yusra

Mardini's dad was a swimming coach who started teaching her to swim when she was just four. Serena Williams's father started even earlier: he wrote a plan for Serena's tennis training before she was even born!

Older siblings also played an important role for many of these Olympians. Megan Rapinoe used to watch her older brother play soccer and copied all his moves. When Yusra Mardini was little, her big sister Sara led the way at the pool—and when war came to their country, she led Yusra to safety in Europe as well.

Yusra wasn't the only athlete who had to overcome difficult circumstances on her way to the Olympics. Wilma Rudolph survived polio and had to learn to walk again before she could run. Jesse Owens faced racist laws and attitudes as a child, as a college student, and at the 1936 Olympic Games in Nazi Germany. Wheelchair racer Tatyana McFadden spent her first five years in a Russian orphanage, where she didn't have access to a wheelchair. And Gertrude Ederle grew up in a time when girls weren't encouraged to do sports at all—and when women had to wear long skirts and stockings to swim!

As kids, these future Olympians didn't all start out looking like stars. At Michael Phelps's first swimming lesson, he threw a tantrum because he didn't want to get his face wet. High jumper Dick Fosbury was

mocked for his unconventional style. And Naomi Osaka
didn't particularly like hitting tennis balls—she just
wanted to beat her older sister!

Although it takes a lot of hard work and
commitment to get to the Olympics, these athletes
didn't always feel like practicing. Simone Biles was torn
between her love of gymnastics and her desire to go to
school and hang out with her friends. Serena Williams
sometimes hit her tennis ball over the fence on purpose,
so she'd have an excuse to take a break. Usain Bolt used
to skip after-school practices to go to the arcade.

In the end, they all had the determination to keep
going, even when the odds seemed stacked against

them. They made it to the Summer Olympic and
Paralympic Games. They won medals, shattered
records, broke new ground, and used their voices to
speak up for what mattered to them.

And every one of them was once a kid who had a
dream—and dared to follow it.

PART

ONE

RACING AHEAD

★ ★ ★ BATTLING ★ ★ ★

PREJUDICE,

★ ★ OVERCOMING ★ ★

OBSTACLES,

AND CHALLENGING

UNFAIR LAWS,

THESE

TRACK STARS

DEFIED EXPECTATIONS

and became the

FASTEST ATHLETES
IN THE WORLD.

Jesse Owens

Fighting the Wind

One of the greatest athletes of all time, Jesse Owens made headlines around the world when he won four gold medals in track and field events at the 1936 Olympics in Berlin. If it wasn't for a teacher's mistake, the name in those headlines would have been a different one!

Jesse Owens was born in the small town of Oakville, Alabama, in 1913. His full name was James Cleveland Owens, and he was the youngest of the ten children in his family. His parents, Henry and Mary Emma, were sharecroppers, farming land they rented from white landowners whom they paid with a share of the crops. Their home was tiny, with no electricity or heating, and they had barely enough money for basic necessities like clothing.

The early 1900s were a difficult time for Black people in the American South: racism was widespread and racial discrimination was enforced by the government. Under a system known as segregation, Black people were kept apart from white people in shops and theaters and made to use separate restrooms and drinking fountains. They had little access to education, few opportunities for employment, and poor medical care.

James—or J. C., as he was usually called—was small for his age and often got sick with fevers and coughs. One of his earliest memories was when he was five and noticed a growth on his chest. Unable to afford to a doctor, his mother operated on him and removed it herself!

But despite his bad health, the family's poverty, and the racism that surrounded them, J. C.'s early childhood was mostly happy. J. C. swam and fished in a pond and went possum hunting with his brothers and their dogs, often staying out beside a campfire until sunrise.

Religion was important to J. C.'s parents, who were devout Baptists. J. C.'s father, Henry, was a deacon at the Oakville Missionary Baptist Church, just up the street from where the Owens family lived, and J. C.'s mother, Mary Emma, made J. C. and his siblings learn a different Bible verse every week. The Oakville Missionary Baptist Church was a small, shabby building that doubled as a school for the local Black children. If the school was open, J. C. could attend classes—but education took second place to farming, and during his early school years, J. C. barely learned to read and write. "We could only go to school when there wasn't anything else going on," he explained.

J. C. spent most of his time outdoors. In addition to their work farming in the fields, his family grew corn, beans, squash, tomatoes, and onions in their garden, and J. C. and the other children often picked fruit from nearby orchards. Much of the time, J. C. was free to play with other kids who lived nearby. He enjoyed keep-away, tag, and hide-and-seek—in fact, he enjoyed any game that involved running! "I always loved running," he said. "I loved it because it was something you could do all by yourself, all under your own power. You could go in any direction, fast or slow as you wanted, fighting the wind if you felt like it, seeking out new sights just on the strength of your feet and the courage of your lungs."

When J. C. was nine years old, his family moved north. This was part of a larger movement of people known as the Great Migration: large numbers of Black people fled the poverty, racism, and violence in the South and moved to the North, settling in the country's largest cities in hopes of greater freedom, more economic opportunities, and better lives for their families. J. C.'s older sister, Lillie, was the first in his family to go, traveling to Cleveland, Ohio. J. C.'s father and two of his brothers soon followed. Meanwhile, back in Alabama, Mary Emma sold the family's possessions and bought train tickets for the rest of the family. When J. C. asked his mother where the train was going, she told him it was taking them all to a better life.

J. C.'s parents found a house on the east side of

Cleveland and J. C. began attending Bolton Elementary School. On his first day, when he told the teacher his name was J. C., she misheard him. "Jesse Owens?" she said. "Yes ma'am, Jesse Owens," he said, not wanting to correct her. From then on, he went by Jesse!

Unlike the schools in the South, Bolton Elementary was integrated, with Black children and white children attending classes together. The principal assumed that Jesse couldn't read or write and put him into first grade with students three years younger than he was. Jesse could barely fit in the tiny desk! He was quickly moved up a grade, but for the rest of his time in school Jesse was two years older than his classmates. Still, he made friends easily.

When Jesse began attending Fairmount Junior High, he met a teacher named Charles Riley. Mr. Riley was the school's track coach, and he quickly spotted Jesse's extraordinary athletic potential. He asked Jesse if he'd like to join the track team, and Jesse said yes, agreeing to practice with Mr. Riley for an hour and a half after school every day. Jesse walked off, excited, and then he remembered something: he had to work after school! He had two jobs, delivering groceries and working in a greenhouse, and his family depended on the money he earned. He raced after Mr. Riley to explain. "That's no problem," Mr. Riley said—and he agreed to coach Jesse first thing in the morning, before school began.

Jesse had to work very hard. He spent many hours in the gym or sprinting on the muddy track in the school field while Mr. Riley shouted instructions to him: "Knees up! Head up! Watch your form!" Jesse enjoyed the training. He loved running, and Mr. Riley had become more than just a coach: he was also an important mentor for Jesse, who thrived on the extra attention.

When Jesse was fifteen and in eighth grade, Mr. Riley organized a one-hundred-yard race on the sidewalk. Wearing the tennis shoes his teacher had given him, Jesse lined up with the other students. "On your marks . . . ready . . . set . . . go!" Mr. Riley shouted.

And they were off. Jesse ran as fast as he could, and when he reached the finish line, well ahead of the others, Mr. Riley was staring at his stopwatch in astonishment. He had expected Jesse to win, but the time his stopwatch was showing seemed impossible: 11 seconds! "I must have punched it too soon," he said. There was no way a 15-year-old kid in cheap shoes could possibly run a hundred yards that fast. After all, the world record for that distance—set by adult sprinters, the fastest in the world, wearing proper gear and running on a real track—was 9.6 seconds. The next day, Mr. Riley timed Jesse again—using a different stopwatch, in case the first one hadn't been accurate— and again, Jesse ran a hundred yards in 11 seconds.

Jesse's first real race was over a longer distance, a quarter mile, but he took off as if it was a sprint, running at top speed. Before the finish line, other runners began overtaking him, and Jesse finished fourth. He felt like he had let his coach down—but Mr. Riley surprised him. He said he would pick Jesse up at his house the next day at one o'clock. "Where are we going?" Jesse asked. "We're going to watch the best runners in the whole world," Mr. Riley told him.

Jesse thought he was going to see one of the runners he admired, but Mr. Riley drove him to a very different kind of racetrack. To Jesse's surprise, they spent the day watching horses! Jesse noticed how effortlessly the horses galloped and how beautifully they moved. Mr. Riley pointed out something else: the horses didn't try to impress anyone. They just ran.

Not long after this, fifteen-year-old Jesse did have
the chance to meet one of his heroes: the sprinter
Charles Paddock, who had won Olympic gold and silver
medals in 1920 and again in 1924. It made Jesse's own
dream feel more possible. Mr. Riley kept encouraging
him too, inviting him home for meals and forming a
friendship that went beyond the track. When Jesse's
father was injured in an accident the following year, it
was Mr. Riley's support that helped Jesse stay in school,
and when, in the fall of 1930, Jesse transferred to East
Technical High School, Mr. Riley continued coaching
him. Jesse later said that Mr. Riley had been like a
father to him. In his last year of high school, Jesse won
seventy-five of the seventy-nine races he ran in—and
when he went to college at Ohio State University, he

continued racing. It wasn't easy: Black students weren't allowed to live in the school's dorms, so Jesse had to live off campus. When Jesse traveled with the track team, racist segregation laws meant he had to stay at separate Blacks-only hotels and eat at Blacks-only restaurants. Between training for track and working to pay for school, Jesse had little time to study. If his grades didn't improve, he was told, he wouldn't be allowed to compete!

Luckily, Jesse managed to bring his grades up—just in time to stun the world with an almost unbelievable performance. At a 1935 event in Michigan, he broke three world records and tied a fourth—in less than an hour! More than eight decades later, this feat is still widely referred to as the greatest forty-five minutes in sports history.

When the next Summer Olympics came around in 1936, Jesse was ready. But there was a problem: the Olympics were being held in Berlin, Germany, and Hitler and the Nazi party had taken over the German government. The Nazis considered Black people, along with Jewish people, to be inferior to white Germans, and they were passing laws that harmed Jewish people and other minorities.

Some Americans wanted to boycott the Olympics, so an American Olympic official flew to Germany to investigate. Of course, he saw only what the Nazi government wanted him to see, and he wrongly concluded that no discrimination was happening. The Americans decided to send a track team—and Jesse Owens was on his way to Germany.

In Berlin, Jesse's Olympic performance was breathtaking. He won four gold medals: long jump, the 100- and 200-meter dashes, and the 4x100-meter relay. Jesse was the most successful athlete at the Berlin Summer Games—and the first American to win four gold medals in track and field at a single Olympics. His success, and the success of other Black American athletes, helped to undermine the racist messages the Nazi party was attempting to spread throughout the Games.

When Jesse returned to America, he was invited to a celebration in his honor at New York's Waldorf-Astoria hotel—and discovered that he would have to take the freight elevator to get to the event. "I came back to my native country and I couldn't ride in the front of the bus. I had to go to the back door," he said. His incredible athletic achievements at the Olympics had done little to change his status as a Black man and he continued to be frustrated by the ongoing racial segregation in his country.

The 1936 US Olympic team was invited to a competition in Sweden, but Jesse, who had very little money, decided to stay in the United States and accept some well-paid endorsement offers and speaking engagements instead. US athletic officials were angry and immediately took away his status as an amateur athlete. This meant Jesse could no longer compete in events like the Olympics, which were only for amateurs, and it wasn't long before the endorsement offers ended and he was broke again. After that, Jesse worked various jobs—as a gas station attendant, at a playground, managing a dry cleaning business—and he began challenging sprinters to race him for cash. He even raced against motorbikes, cars, trucks, and horses! "I had four gold medals, but you can't eat gold medals," he said.

But Jesse never gave up, and by the 1950s he had become a successful and inspiring public speaker. He received many awards, from the Presidential Medal of Freedom to the US Library of Congress's Living Legend Award. In the words of President Jimmy Carter, "Perhaps no athlete better symbolized the human struggle against tyranny, poverty, and racial bigotry."

Wilma Rudolph

The Feeling of Freedom

When Wilma Rudolph was twenty, newspaper headlines called her the fastest woman on earth after she became the first American woman to win three gold medals in track and field at a single Olympics. But before she could run, she first had to recover from an illness that left her unable to walk.

Wilma Rudolph was born on June 23, 1940, in St. Bethlehem, Tennessee. Her mother, Blanche, worked as a maid, and her father, Ed, was a railway porter. Wilma was the twentieth of twenty-two children from her father's two marriages. Soon after Wilma's birth, her family moved to Clarksville, Tennessee. With so many children to support, it was hard to make ends meet.

Wilma had been born early, and like most premature babies, she was tiny—weighing just four and a half pounds. She was often sick, fighting one infection after another: measles and mumps, chicken pox and whooping cough, pneumonia and scarlet fever. Today, most of these illnesses can be prevented by vaccination, but when Wilma was a child, they were common and could be very dangerous.

Wilma survived them all, but when she was four or five, she became sicker than she had ever been before. She was diagnosed with polio. For the first half of the 1900s—until the creation of a vaccine—polio loomed as a terrifying threat, with epidemics breaking out across the country. Many parents kept their children indoors during the summer months when the risk was highest. Thousands of people died of polio during the 1940s, most of them children—and every year, more than 35,000 survivors were left paralyzed.

Wilma's mother cared for her daughter at home. There was a local hospital, but she couldn't take her daughter there; the 1940s were a time of racial segregation in the southern US, and the hospital didn't provide care for Black children.

Wilma survived, but the virus left her left leg and foot paralyzed. "I was six years old before I realized that there was something wrong with me. . . . I [had] this crooked left leg, and my left foot was turned inward," she said. For two years, she couldn't walk. "My doctor told me I would never walk again," she recalled. "My mother told me I would. I believed my mother."

It wasn't easy, but eventually Wilma's mother found somewhere that would help her child: a Black medical college in Nashville. Founded in 1876, Meharry Medical College was the first medical school for African Americans in the South. Twice a week, Wilma and her mother rode the bus to the city. With exercises and massage, and the support of a special shoe and a brace on her left leg, Wilma began relearning how to walk.

Between treatments, her older brothers and sisters cared for her at home. They helped her exercise, and four times a day, they massaged her leg. Wilma missed kindergarten and first grade because of her illness, but when she was seven, she began attending classes at Cobb Elementary School in Clarksville. Her condition had improved and she could walk again, but she still couldn't run and play like the other kids. Over the next few years, with her family's support, Wilma continued to recover. She grew stronger and no longer needed the brace, and by the time she was ready for high school, she had made a full recovery.

In addition to restricting which hospitals people could be treated at, segregation laws at that time also required Black children and white children to attend separate schools. Wilma and her older sister Yvonne attended Bart High School, a school for Black students. Yvonne was very athletic, and the basketball coach wanted her on the team, but the girls' dad knew Wilma wanted to play too. Her brothers had taught her basketball and played with her in the backyard. Their dad told the coach to take both girls, and the coach agreed. To his surprise, Wilma proved to be not just capable but extremely talented. In her second year on the team, she scored 803 points, setting a record for high school girls' basketball in Tennessee! The team's coach, C. C. Gray, called her Skeeter—slang for mosquito. "You're little, you're fast, and you always get in my way," he said.

While playing for her high school basketball team, Wilma was spotted by Ed Temple, the track and field coach from Tennessee State University. Wilma was only in tenth grade, but the coach could see that she was a natural athlete and thought she had potential in track. He invited her to join his summer training program at the university.

After that summer's training camp, Wilma competed in an Amateur Athletic Union track meet in Philadelphia—and she won all nine of the events she entered! Although she was still a high school student, she continued training at Tennessee State University, and she raced with their women's track team, the Tigerbelles. "I ran and ran and ran every day, and I acquired this sense of determination, this sense of spirit that I would never, never give up, no matter what else happened," she said.

Just two years later, Wilma and five other members of the Tigerbelles qualified for the 1956 Olympics Games in Melbourne, Australia. Only sixteen years old, Wilma was the team's youngest member. She took part in the 4x100-meter relay, a 4-person event in which each member runs 100 meters, passing a baton to the next runner. Wilma ran the third leg of the relay, helping the American team to win a bronze medal. It was a remarkable achievement for anyone, and almost unbelievable for a young woman who, just a few years earlier, had needed the support of a leg brace to walk. When she returned home, Wilma showed her school friends her bronze medal. She was determined to win a gold one at the next Olympic Games.

In 1958, Wilma enrolled as a student at Tennessee State University and continued training with Ed Temple as her coach. She took real joy in her sport. "I loved the feeling of freedom in running, the fresh air, the feeling that the only person I'm competing with is me," she said.

Wilma may have been competing with herself, but she was also beating everyone else! She qualified for the 1960 Summer Olympics, and during the qualification races, she also set a new world record in the 200 meters. The previous record had been unbroken for eight years.

The 1960 Summer Olympics were held in Rome, Italy, and it was incredibly hot! The day before Wilma's first race, she stepped in a hole near the practice track and twisted her ankle. It swelled up and looked bruised, but that didn't stop Wilma. She raced in three events— the 100- and 200-meter races, as well as the 4x100- meter relay—and she won them all. It was the first time an American woman had won three gold medals in track and field at a single Olympics—and to make it even more impressive, she won all three events in record-breaking times. The crowd went wild. "People were jumping all over me, putting microphones into my face, pounding my back, and I couldn't believe it," she wrote later.

Wilma was hailed by the media as "the Tornado," "the Black Gazelle," and "the Flash." She was called the fastest woman on earth and named the United Press International Athlete of the Year. Just twenty years old, she was suddenly famous. When she came home, her hometown of Clarksville celebrated "Welcome Wilma Day"—and Wilma insisted that if there was going to be a parade, it needed to be integrated so that Black people and white people could celebrate together. More than a thousand people showed up! It was the first fully integrated municipal event in the city's history.

Wilma surprised everyone when, just two years later, she announced her retirement. She wanted to stop racing while she was at the top of her game—like Jesse Owens, her childhood hero, had done. Wilma said, "The feeling of accomplishment welled up inside of me, three Olympic gold medals. I knew that was something nobody could ever take away from me, ever."

Soon after her retirement, Wilma traveled to West Africa as the US representative at the 1963 Friendship Games in Dakar, Senegal. These games later became known as the Pan African Games. While in West Africa, Wilma also traveled to Ghana, Guinea, Mali, and Upper Volta (the previous name for the country now called Burkina Faso), attending sporting events, meeting athletes, and visiting schools.

Wilma was an international star—one of the most visible Black women in the United States and around the world. After she returned to the United States, she took part in a civil rights protest in Clarksville to desegregate one of the city's restaurants. She kept on attending protests, and soon the city's mayor announced that all restaurants and public facilities would be fully integrated.

After her Olympic victory, Wilma went back to Tennessee State University and completed a bachelor's degree in elementary education. She went on to have a career in teaching and coaching, even working for a while at the elementary and high schools she had attended as a kid. She was voted into the Black Athletes

Hall of Fame and the National Track and Field Hall of Fame. An important figure in civil rights and women's rights, Wilma has inspired generations of Black women athletes—including Florence Griffith Joyner. In 1988, when Florence—known as Flo Jo—became the next woman to win three Olympic gold medals, Wilma was watching. "It was a great thrill for me to see," she said. "I thought I'd never get to see that. Florence Griffith Joyner—every time she ran, I ran." It was a legacy she was very proud of.

Usain Bolt

> ## The Fastest Kid in Jamaica

Usain Bolt may be the fastest runner ever. An eight-time Olympic gold medalist, he holds the world records for the 100- and 200-meter sprints—but as a twelve-year-old, he used to skip practices to play *Mario Kart* at the local arcade!

Usain Bolt was born on August 21, 1986, in Jamaica. His home was in a small village in a sunny valley within Trelawny Parish. His father, Wellesley, had two other kids—Usain's younger brother, Sadiki, and his older sister, Christine. Usain's mom was named Jennifer and he was her only child.

Even as an infant, Usain was full of energy. Once he learned to crawl, he was unstoppable: he wanted to go everywhere and climb everything! "I wouldn't sit still; I couldn't stand in one place for longer than a second," he said. Finally, his exhausted parents took him to the doctor. The doctor said that Usain was hyperactive but that he would outgrow it eventually.

Living in a farming community, Usain grew up

eating lots of fresh food like yams, bananas, oranges, coconut, mangoes, berries, and guava. "Everything grew in and around the backyard," he recalled. "If my stomach rumbled I would find a tree and pick fruits." The forests around his home made a wonderful playground for an active kid.

When he was five or six, Usain discovered the sport of cricket. He and his friends played on the street, sometimes even making their own balls from rubber bands or old string. For a wicket, they used wood from banana trees, piles of stones, or cardboard. Cricket was popular at school too; Usain attended Waldensia Primary in the nearby town of Sherwood Content. Usain's dad, who was loving but also very strict, insisted that Usain say good morning to every single adult he saw on his way to school.

Usain was a polite and confident boy who made friends easily. One of them, Nugent Walker Junior, lived close by and the two boys became best friends. Nugent's nickname was NJ, and for a while, people started calling Usain VJ. He wasn't sure why, but he liked it— partly because he was tired of people pronouncing Usain incorrectly!

Usain did well in school in the early years. He had a competitive streak and was determined to solve math problems faster than NJ. "I loved to compete," he said. "And I really hated losing." But his real passion was for sports. He was fast, and he had the advantage of being taller than most kids his age. Despite being younger than most of the players on his school cricket team, he was soon batting for the squad.

When he was eight, one of his teachers, Mr. Nugent, noticed what a fast runner Usain was. Usain didn't think he was all that fast, because there was another kid, Ricardo, who always beat him. So he shrugged off his teacher's suggestion that he try running—until Mr. Nugent bribed him with the offer of a special lunch if he could outrun Ricardo in the 100-meter race at school sports day. Jerk chicken, potatoes, rice, and peas? That sounded good to Usain.

All the students came out to watch the big race. On the sports field, a running track had been made by scorching the grass with burning gasoline to create black lines between the lanes. Usain was nervous—but determined to win. By the time he reached the finish line, he was a long way ahead of Ricardo. He was the fastest kid at his school, and he felt great.

After that, Usain started competing with kids from other schools. His house was filling up with medals and trophies! In Jamaica, track and field was hugely important—much like football and basketball at many schools in the United States. William Knibbs School, a short drive away, had a strong reputation for athletics. One of the former students had even run at the Olympics! When the principal saw Usain run, he offered him a scholarship, and so, at age eleven, Usain began attending school at William Knibbs.

Usain's parents were happy; they wanted their son to have every opportunity, but they couldn't have afforded expensive school fees. To Usain's shock, his new school wouldn't let him play cricket. They wanted him to focus on running. Usain was disappointed, but his dad pointed out that in some ways, running might be better than a team sport: "in track and field you're the boss of yourself," he told his son.

Usain tried various races, from short sprints to longer distances. He was tall for the 100 meters—it took him too long to get his body upright coming out of the starting blocks—and long-distance running was too much work. The 200- and 400-meter races seemed just right, taking advantage of his long stride, his speed, and his stamina. At those distances, Usain was so fast, his coaches could hardly believe it.

In fact, he had so much natural talent that winning races wasn't difficult for him at all—and that, in a way, created its own problems! Because he didn't have to train hard to win, his technique was sloppy. "If I'd flapped my arms a bit more, I probably would have taken flight," he admitted. He started skipping evening practices and heading to the local arcade instead. Using the coins his mom gave him to buy lunch, he'd play *Mario Kart* and *Mortal Kombat* for hours. "Most evenings my hands would hurt from the joystick because I'd played for too long," he said.

Usain wasn't very motivated in the classroom either. His father was worried. If Usain failed a year, he'd have to repeat it, and that would cost money. Besides, Usain's dad pointed out, a career as a runner might not work out. Usain needed an education to fall back on. Determined to tackle what he saw as his son's laziness, he began waking Usain up at 5:30 every morning. But after his dad left for work, Usain's mom let him go back to sleep until the last possible minute—and then called him a cab so that he wouldn't be late to school.

Eventually, Usain encountered a runner who was faster than him. At the Regional Championships, known as Champs, a boy called Keith Spence beat him repeatedly. Usain didn't like that at all. Vowing to win his next race, he began training more seriously—and he saw a video that changed everything. It was footage of the 1996 Olympic Games in Atlanta, where Michael Johnson won gold medals in both the 200- and 400-meter races. *I want to be an Olympic gold medalist,* Usain thought as he watched.

Michael Johnson ran with an unusual upright posture and Usain was fascinated. He began watching videos of other great Jamaican athletes such as Herb McKenley, Arthur Wint, and Don Quarrie, and he realized that he had a lot to learn. He practiced his corners, keeping closer to the inside of the track, and worked to improve his running technique.

At the next Regional Championships, Usain was determined to beat his rival. When the starting gun fired, Keith flew out of the blocks ahead of Usain—but once Usain hit his stride, he powered past him, crossing the finish line with a huge lead. Victory!

The win gave Usain the chance to represent his country at the 2001 CARIFTA Games, a Caribbean-wide competition held in Barbados. It was his first time leaving Jamaica, and he was homesick—but soon he was traveling again, to an international youth championship in Hungary. Usain found it very cold and thought the food was weird, but strangest of all was the bottled water. He'd never encountered fizzy water before!

A year later, Usain broke several CARIFTA records, earning the nickname Lighting Bolt. The World Juniors were held in Kingston, Jamaica, that year, and the huge crowd made Usain so nervous that he almost put his shoes on the wrong feet! Despite his fears—and despite being only fifteen, several years younger than his competitors—he won the men's 200 meters.

At seventeen, Usain moved to Kingston to train full-time. It was a difficult year: Usain was injured, and then he learned that he had scoliosis, a curvature of the spine. He did badly in some races, and the media criticized him for going to parties and eating fast food. But Usain didn't quit. He found a new coach and trained hard, and by the time he was twenty, he was winning international competitions.

People had always told Usain he was too tall to be a sprinter, but he was about to prove them all wrong. He persuaded his coach to let him try the shorter 100-meter races as well as the 200-meters—and in 2008, he won his first Olympic gold medals in Beijing, China. Four years later, he won three more golds (in the 100- and 200-meter sprints and the 4x100 relay) at the Olympics in London—and earned a Guinness World Record as the first athlete to win the 100- and 200-meter sprint at two Olympics in a row! Four years later, in 2016, he did it again, winning gold in all three events at the Olympic Games in Rio de Janeiro, Brazil.

An eleven-time world champion, Usain Bolt is considered the greatest sprinter of all time.

Tatyana McFadden

The World's Fastest Woman

Wheelchair racer Tatyana McFadden is known as the fastest woman in the world. She has won twenty Paralympic medals, eight of them gold. But as a teenager, she had to fight for her right to be part of her school track team.

Tatyana was born on April 21, 1989, in St. Petersburg, Russia, with a condition called spina bifida. Her spine hadn't fully closed before her birth, which left her paralyzed from the waist down. Babies born with spina bifida need surgery as soon as possible, but Tatyana had to wait three weeks. It was a miracle she survived.

At the time, there was little awareness about disability in Russia. In fact, the government insisted there were no disabled people in the country! Without help, Tatyana's birth mother couldn't care for her. So Tatyana was placed in an orphanage.

Tatyana slept in a room with a dozen other children. Each morning, they were all washed with cold water and dressed. One day Tatyana's clothes might be too small, the next day, they might be too big. "We all shared the same clothes," Tatyana said.

For the children in Baby House #13, there was little medical care and no school. Often, there was not even enough food: Tatyana and the other children mostly ate porridge, cabbage, and potatoes. Between meals, the children were put on mats on the floor, or left in their cribs. There were no books, no television, few toys to play with—and there was no wheelchair for Tatyana. "The only way to get around was that I scooted around the floor using my hands as my legs," Tatyana said. "I was a very stubborn child." By the time she was five, she had figured out how to turn herself upside down and walk on her hands!

The director of the orphanage, Natalya Vasalya, told Tatyana that she wanted to find a home for her, but Tatyana was confused: wasn't this her home? Then, in 1993, an American named Deborah McFadden visited the orphanage. Deborah was the Commissioner of Disabilities for the US Department of Health and Human Services, and she was visiting many orphanages in Russia as part of her work.

When she came to Baby House #13, she spotted Tatyana, wearing a bow in her hair that was at least as big as her head. Deborah invited the girl to sit on her lap, and Tatyana crawled over and immediately started pointing and asking questions about Deborah's camera. Tatyana was speaking Russian, and Deborah was speaking English—but Deborah felt an unexpected connection to the bright-eyed little girl who seemed to understand everything. That night, back at her hotel, she couldn't stop thinking about her.

So Deborah visited the orphanage again and again. She brought clothes, toys, and candy—and a wheelchair! Deborah lifted Tatyana onto the seat and showed her how to use her hands to turn the wheels. Then she took her outside to let Tatyana try going faster. Tatyana felt like she was flying! It was the first time she had been outside the iron fence that surrounded the orphanage.

When Tatyana was five, Deborah and her partner, Bridget O'Shaughnessy, decided to adopt the young girl. Tatyana was happy, but she was also scared. The world outside the orphanage was unfamiliar, and leaving the people she'd known all her life was hard.

Tatyana and Deborah took a taxi and then an overnight train to Moscow. The next day was full of new experiences: so many buildings, sidewalks packed with people, and carts filled with flowers and candy! "In that one afternoon, I had my first taste of ice cream, soda pop, and chocolate," Tatyana said.

Then they flew to America—and arriving at Deborah and Bridget's home in Baltimore brought more new experiences. Tatyana had a warm bath—with scented bubbles and floating boats and ducks. And the next morning, instead of porridge for breakfast, she could choose from tiny colorful boxes, each filled with a different kind of cereal. There was fresh fruit, toast, and jam. Tatyana could hardly believe it was all for her.

Deborah and Bridget decided to throw their new daughter a birthday party to welcome her, although her actual birthday had been months earlier. There was a cake with six candles, and gifts wrapped up with ribbons and bows. Tatyana was surprised when the guests introduced themselves: they all had the last name McFadden. "I McFadden too!" she exclaimed. It took her a moment to realize that all these people were her new relatives.

Tatyana's first months in Baltimore included many visits to doctors. Her legs were stiff and bent behind her, so she had operations to straighten them. This meant she could sit in her shiny pink wheelchair more comfortably—and just as importantly to Tatyana, she could wear shoes!

Her parents (she called Deborah Mom and Bridget Momma) thought that physical activity would help her get stronger, so they enrolled her in the Bennett Blazers. This was a sports club for kids with disabilities. Tatyana tried ice hockey, basketball, skiing, archery, and wheelchair racing. "The moment I sat in that racing chair, I knew it was for me," she said. "I could go really fast." When she was in the racing chair, Tatyana felt like she could go forever.

Tatyana's mothers encouraged her to try things on her own. Deborah knew what it was like to be seen as less capable than she was. As a university student, she had developed an illness that meant she needed to use an electric wheelchair for several years. She had hated

the way people treated her as if she couldn't do things—
and she wanted Tatyana to know she could do anything
she put her mind to.

Tatyana never seemed to doubt that she could!
When a swimming instructor didn't think she would be
able to swim, Tatyana fearlessly jumped in the pool. "Ya
sama!" she shouted. *Ya sama* is a Russian phrase that
literally translates as "I, myself," but it can also mean, "I
can do it."

When Tatyana was ten, something exciting
happened: Deborah and Bridget adopted a three-year-
old girl, Hannah, from Albania. Tatyana remembers
meeting her at the airport when she arrived. "I put her
on my lap and tried to talk to her," Tatyana said. "She
was very shy, so I made all these silly gestures." Back at

home, Tatyana read her new younger sister stories, dressed her up, and put bows in her hair.

Tatyana knew she wanted to be a professional athlete, and her mothers supported her fully. Bridget even rode her bike alongside Tatyana's racing chair when she was training. At thirteen, Tatyana broke the world record for her age group in the 100-meter sprint—and at school, when the kids were asked to write down their goals, she wrote, "Going to be in the Olympics in Athens in 2004." And she was! At fifteen, the youngest member of the US Paralympic team, Tatyana won two medals, silver in the 100 meters and bronze in the 200 meters.

But at her high school, Tatyana was encountering unexpected obstacles. She wanted to join the track team, but the school wouldn't let her. She was too fast, they said, and her chair posed a danger to the other runners. If she wanted to race, she would have to go around and around on an empty track, alone.

As a same-sex couple, Tatyana's mothers had experienced discrimination themselves. So when Tatyana came home, devastated by the school's decision, Deborah suggested that they could sue the school—not for money, but for the right for students with disabilities to take part in sports alongside their classmates. Tatyana agreed. She saw it as an opportunity to make things better for the young athletes with disabilities who might come along after her—including her sister, Hannah, an amputee who walked with a prosthetic leg. "I didn't want her to go through the same experience of having to fight for this," Tatyana said.

The school officials were angry, and so were some of Tatyana's classmates and their parents. "Every track meet that I went to they were always booing," Tatyana recalled. "But on the inside I just knew this was the right thing to do."

She won, and the legal battle led to a new law in Maryland: the Fitness and Athletics Equity for Students with Disabilities Act, also known as Tatyana's Law. In 2013, that law became federal; all schools in the United States had to ensure that students with disabilities had equal opportunities to compete in school athletics. Tatyana got to see the impact of her activism when Hannah reached high school. "No one thought of her as anyone different," Tatyana said. "They just thought, 'Oh, cool. She's in a wheelchair. And she's on my track team. That's awesome.'"

Meanwhile, the family had grown again; Deborah and Bridget adopted a third child, Ruthi, from Albania. Tatyana's track career had taken off too: she won race after race at the Paralympics in Beijing, London, and Rio de Janeiro. At a World Championship event, she made history when she won races at every distance from 100 meters to 5,000 meters, becoming the first athlete to win six gold medals at one competition. Tatyana started competing in marathons as well; she holds a record of twenty-four titles in the six World Marathon Majors. In 2013 she scored a Grand Slam by winning marathons in Boston, Chicago, New York City, and London in the same year—a feat she has since repeated four times! In 2017, Tatyana shared the winner's podium with her training partner and best friend—her sister, Hannah, also a world-class wheelchair racer.

Tatyana is just as powerful off the track, as an advocate for people—and especially children—with disabilities. She coproduced and starred in *Rising Phoenix*, a Netflix documentary about Paralympic athletes. "We're all fighting a bigger fight," she said. "We're all fighting for equality globally." That includes the battle for equal pay for athletes with disabilities; thanks to activists like Tatyana, the Tokyo 2020 Summer Games became the first time Paralympians were awarded the same prize money as Olympians. Tatyana was there to celebrate this victory—and to win three more Olympic medals!

Tatyana has even written a book for children about her life. Its title, *Ya Sama!*, is based on her motto: I can do it.

Like the Olympics, the Paralympic Games feature elite athletes from around the world, and many of the sports are the same: track and field, swimming, gymnastics, fencing, and more. What makes the Paralympics different is that all the athletes have physical disabilities.

The history of the Paralympics begins in July 1948. Sir Ludwig Guttman, a Jewish German doctor who had come to England as a refugee, organized a wheelchair sports competition at Stoke Mandeville Hospital. Sixteen ex-soldiers with spinal cord injuries took part. Four years later, the event was held again, and this time athletes from the Netherlands and Israel joined in, making it the first international event of its kind.

The first official Paralympic Games were held in 1960 in Rome, Italy. Today, Paralympic Games are held every two years, in the same host cities and athletic venues as the Summer and Winter Olympics. The Games have played an important role in challenging perceptions of disability in countries around the world.

TWO

MAKING HISTORY

BEING THE

★ ★ ★ FIRST ★ ★ ★

isn't always easy,

BUT THESE OLYMPIANS

BROKE NEW GROUND

ON THEIR WAY TO

THE PODIUM

AND PAVED

THE WAY

FOR THOSE WHO
WOULD FOLLOW.

Dick Fosbury

Daring to Be Different

When Dick Fosbury was a teenager, people laughed at the unconventional way he cleared the high jump bar. He went on to win Olympic gold—and along the way, he forever changed his sport.

His full name was Richard Douglas Fosbury, but he was always known as Dick. He was born in Portland, Oregon, on March 6, 1947, and grew up in the town of Medford. His father, Doug, worked as a salesman at a truck store, and his mother, Helen, was a bookkeeper. Dick was their oldest kid; his sister, Gail, was born when he was three, and his brother, Greg, came along a year later. Dick's classmates from Roosevelt Elementary described him as a laid-back and lighthearted kid who loved comic books and could sometimes be goofy—like the time he put Limburger cheese on the radiator in the school cafeteria to see how it would smell!

In Medford, track and field was even more popular than baseball. Dick's father had been on the track team in high school, and Dick started getting involved when he was just eleven. He wasn't great at running or throwing, so he decided to focus on high jump. The following year, when his family moved to a new house in Medford, Dick's father built him a high jump bar with a sawdust landing pit in the back yard!

The Fosburys were an active family: Helen played piano, Doug went bowling, and they both enjoyed square dancing. In the summers, the family took vacations together on the coast or at a nearby lake. They had a terrier named Wags, and on Friday nights, they played board games like Monopoly and Yahtzee.

But when Dick was fourteen, everything changed. One evening a few days before Dick's first day of ninth grade at Hedrick Junior High, he and his brother, Greg, were riding their bicycles when Greg was struck by a car and killed. The driver took off, but he later turned himself in to the police and admitted that he had been drinking.

The accident was the fault of the drunk driver—but Dick blamed himself. If he'd ridden behind his brother, he thought, his brother would have been safe and Dick would have been the one who was hit. A year later, unable to find a path through their grief together, Dick's parents divorced. It was a difficult time for Dick, who had very little support in dealing with either his brother's death or his parents' divorce. In need of a distraction, he turned his focus to high jumping.

A few months before the accident, the phys ed teacher at Dick's school had demonstrated the two ways to clear a high jump bar—the scissors jump and the straddle jump, also known as the western roll or belly roll. When Dick tried the scissors, he performed it differently than his teacher had, jumping off from his right foot instead of his left—but he cleared the bar easily. "He was smooth as silk," one of his classmates recalled. "Like a human gazelle." It was the way Dick had been jumping in his back yard, since he was eleven. But when Dick tried the straddle method, it was a disaster. "Nothing worked," his classmate said. "Dick's arms and legs flew in five different directions, the bar clanged off the standards, and Dick landed on it."

Dick didn't stand out as an athlete when he started at Medford High School. He was tall and skinny—a student that the high school track coach, Coach Benson, later described as "a gangly, gawky, grew-too-fast kid." Dick's father bought him some weights, but Dick didn't really use them. He tried out for football but didn't make the team, and while he enjoyed basketball, he wasn't particularly skilled at the game. Even in track, he wasn't dreaming of being a star. He certainly wasn't thinking about going to the Olympics. "I lived in the moment," he said. Mostly what he liked to do was read comics; his favorites were Superman, Batman, Archie, and Richie Rich.

All the same, being on the track team was incredibly important to him—it was the one place where he felt like he belonged. "All I ever wanted to do was just make the team and stay on the team," he said. At this time, nearly all the jumpers used the straddle jump, so Coach Benson persuaded Dick to use that technique despite his difficulty with it. Dick worked hard, but by the time he was sixteen, he was still unable to jump higher than the 5 feet 4 inches he'd achieved back in ninth grade.

There was a track meet coming up at Grants Pass, and Dick was feeling desperate. Track was competitive at Medford High, and if he didn't improve fast, another student would take his spot on the team. Should he go back to the scissors jump? Coach Benson dismissed that idea; no one did the scissors anymore, he said.

But Dick was persistent, and Coach Benson eventually gave in. After all, it didn't really matter: Dick hadn't qualified to go on to the district level, so this was probably going to be his last competition. "It's your decision," the coach told him. Dick's friend was even more blunt: "Whataya got to lose?" he said.

At Grants Pass, Dick was taken aback to see that the high jump pit was right in the middle of the field—and the stands were full of spectators. The opening height for the bar was 5 feet 4 inches, Dick's all-time best height. He was used to failing to clear the bar, but he did not like the thought of failing in front of such a large audience. The question was, should he risk adding to his embarrassment by attempting the scissors?

He decided to try it on his practice jump. Concentrating hard, Dick ran, jumped—and cleared the bar! Around him, other jumpers were laughing at his outdated style, but he didn't care.

Finally, the competition began. One after another, athletes cleared the bar, every last one of them using the straddle jump. And then it was Dick's turn, and again he used the scissors. He cleared the bar—but he had felt his backside brush against it. *Raise your butt, stupid*, he told himself.

But how could he raise his butt in the middle of an upright scissor jump? He decided he would have to lean backward. He was making it up as he went along, but it worked. The bar was raised two inches and he cleared it again—a new personal best! And then the bar was raised again: 5 feet 8 inches. Dick ran, jumped, leaned back even farther . . . and cleared the bar. Another personal best! He hadn't made a conscious decision to invent a strange new version of the scissors jump—but it was working.

As fans moved closer to watch the few jumpers that were still in the competition, Dick's father overheard some mystified spectators talking about his son's unconventional technique. "Starts out like the old scissors," one guy said. "Not sure what it is after that. Looks like a guy taking a nap on a picnic table with his feet over the edge."

Each jumper had three chances to clear the bar. On his first try, Dick hit it. On his second try, he hit it again. But on his third, he cleared it—at 5 feet 10 inches! A full six inches above the height he'd been stuck at since ninth grade! His jump was disqualified on a technicality, but his team had won, and even without his last jump being scored, Dick had come in fourth place. Coach Benson was impressed—but baffled. "Never seen anything like it," he said.

Soon after this, something happened that allowed Dick to experiment more safely: high jump competitions began using cushions or scraps of foam rubber in landing pits instead of sand or wood chips. Medford High was the first school in the state to have a foam pit, and Dick loved it. He kept practicing his new style and modifying it, going over the bar backward, headfirst and belly to the sky. His sister, Gail, said that when Dick was jumping, he was in his own world.

By twelfth grade, Dick was jumping over 6 feet, but the coaches and other jumpers were skeptical. Some people laughed at him. A local newspaper headline read FOSBURY FLOPS OVER BAR. One reporter said he looked like a fish flopping in a barrel, and another called him the world's laziest high jumper. Still others feared he'd get hurt, landing on his back and shoulders instead of his hands and feet. Gail told him to ignore the doubters and jump the way he wanted. That year, Dick jumped 6 feet 5½ inches and placed second in the state.

In 1965, Dick started at Oregon State University. He

was still figuring out his new style, and it didn't always work out. One time, someone bet him that he couldn't jump over a stuffed leather chair. "Not only did I lose the bet, I also broke my hand in the crash landing," he recalled.

His new coach, Benny Wagner, wanted him to keep practicing more traditional jumps—but when Dick jumped 6 feet 10 inches, smashing the school's high jump record, Coach Wagner began studying Dick's technique and teaching it to the younger athletes.

In 1968, Dick competed at the Summer Olympics in Mexico City. Even in the lead-up to the Games, sports reporters were still seeing him as a funny story rather than as a medal contender. One wrote that he went over the bar "like a guy being pushed out of a 30-story window" and *Sports Illustrated* said he looked like "a two-legged camel"!

Dick defied convention in other ways at the Olympics, too. He didn't like to practice with the other athletes, and he skipped the opening ceremony to take a drive, see the pyramids, and sleep in a van. Nonetheless, he won a gold medal—and he set a new Olympic record of 7 feet 4¼ inches. By the next Olympics, in Munich in 1972, more than half the athletes were copying Dick's jumping style.

Dick Fosbury's determination to do things his own way transformed the high jump, and today nearly all high jumpers use his technique. He named it the Fosbury Flop.

Nadia Comăneci

Dreaming of Somersaults

When Nadia Comăneci was fourteen, she became the first gymnast to score a perfect 10 at the Olympic Games—but if her nonstop energy hadn't gotten her into so much trouble as a little kid, her mom might never have signed her up for gymnastics lessons!

Nadia Elena Comăneci was born in Romania on
November 12, 1961, and grew up in a small village
called Onești. Her father, Gheorghe, was an auto
mechanic, and her mother, Ștefania, worked in an office.
During Nadia's early childhood, a man called Nicolae
Ceaușescu rose to power, becoming the leader of the
Romanian Communist Party and then the country's
president. He was a dictator who caused tremendous
suffering to Romania's people. As Nadia got older, his
government would make her life increasingly difficult—
but as as a child, she knew nothing about her country's
politics.

Nadia was a happy girl who loved playing outside,
visiting her grandparents' farm and digging up carrots

or picking tomatoes to eat. Sometimes she and her grandmother caught fish together. They would put cornmeal inside a hollow ball and wait for the tiny fish to swim inside. Then they'd pull the ball out of the water and fry the trapped fish whole for dinner. Nadia thought they were delicious!

When Nadia was five, her parents had a baby, Adrian. Nadia adored him. He was too small to play with, but Nadia didn't mind; she enjoyed playing alone. She climbed tall trees and swung on their branches. Once she even tried to climb the Christmas tree, but when her parents came home, they found her trapped underneath it—eating the handfuls of candy she'd managed to grab from the top branches!

When roller skates became popular, Nadia wanted a pair. Her mom told her that they couldn't afford them, but Nadia talked her dad into a trip to the store—just to try them on, she said. She laced up the skates and began skating around the store. They let her go so fast! Nadia couldn't bear to give the skates back—so she skated out the door and onto the street. Her father had no choice. He had to buy them. "I have never been able to take no for an answer," Nadia admitted.

When her dad told her that her new bicycle—a birthday gift—wasn't ready to ride, she ignored his warning. "As soon as he left for work, I rode away, losing both pedals and eventually having the bicycle collapse beneath me into a pile of pieces," Nadia said.

Her dad made her wait for a whole week before he put it back together and tightened the screws!

When Nadia was in kindergarten, her mom decided that her daughter needed an outlet for her energy. "Jumping on beds, spending day and night racing around the village, and punching little boys in the nose when they refused to let me play was no longer working for my mother," Nadia said. Her mom took her to a gymnasium filled with equipment—mats, vaults, beams, and parallel bars—and Nadia could hardly wait to try it all out. She started taking gymnastics classes and she loved them. It didn't hurt that her instructor used to give them all a little piece of chocolate at the end of class. Chocolate was a rare treat and Nadia loved it.

When Nadia was six, a man named Bela Karolyi saw her doing cartwheels in the schoolyard and invited her to join his gymnastics school. Six days a week, she did school work for four hours and then four hours of gymnastics. The training was fun. "I could do things that my mom wouldn't let me do at home," she said.

Bela Karolyi ran the school with his wife, Marta. They were very strict and they pushed Nadia hard—but she pushed herself even harder. "If they said twenty-five push-ups, I'd do fifty," Nadia said. When she got her first leotard, she loved it much that she kicked her doll out of her bed and slept with the leotard instead.

Nadia was nine when she went to her first major competition, the 1970 National Championships. She wanted desperately to do well, but with her first leap, she fell off the left side of the beam. She climbed back up—and promptly fell off the other side. "It was my first taste of failure," she said, "and I didn't like it at all." Nadia came away with a thirteenth-place finish—and a determination to do better.

Unlike many young gymnasts, Nadia wasn't dreaming about the competing in Olympics. In fact, she'd never even heard of them! Her family had a tiny black-and-white television, but it only showed the three government-approved channels. So Nadia's dreams weren't about competition or fame, but about skills. "I dreamed of running and twisting and double somersaults," she said.

Nadia's first chance to compete with athletes from other countries was at the 1972 Friendship Cup. She and her teammates were ten years old, and they were shocked to discover that the other gymnasts were all in their late teens and early twenties! Her coaches were surprised too; they had never seen gymnasts from other countries competing and hadn't realized they would be older. But Nadia surprised everyone, beating the best gymnasts in the world to win the all-around gold medal.

When Nadia was thirteen, she went to Norway for the European Women's Artistic Gymnastics Championships, where she won four gold medals. A year later, in 1976, she traveled with her coaches to Canada for the Montreal Olympic Games.

It was only when she arrived that Nadia realized how important the Olympic Games were. "I was flabbergasted," she said. "I was afraid to close my eyes because I didn't want to miss anything." The Olympic Village, where all the athletes stayed, was huge! There were people from all over the world, some of them competing in sports she'd never heard of. Nadia was given matching clothing, hats and pins—and everything was free, including seeing a movie or getting a soft drink or eating all kinds of food. Nadia had never seen pizza before, or peanut butter, or breakfast cereal.

But Nadia wasn't allowed to try new foods, go anywhere alone, or even march in the opening ceremony. She was there for one thing only: to perform perfectly.

Nadia's first routine was on the uneven bars. She thought it went well, but when she looked up at the scoreboard, it read 1.0.

Then one of the judges held up ten fingers. Nadia had scored the first perfect 10 in gymnastics history—and the scoreboard wasn't programmed to show scores higher than 9.9. It was a historic moment, but Nadia barely had time to take it in. "I had to rush off and march to the balance beam for my next routine," she said. Nadia went on to score six more perfect 10s, winning three gold medals and becoming the youngest ever Olympic gymnastics all-around champion.

For Nadia, arriving home was overwhelming. President Ceauşescu saw Nadia's success as a great victory for Romania and the country was celebrating, so when Nadia stepped off the plane, she saw thousands of cheering fans. "It was scary," she said. "Everyone was pushing, pulling, and trying to touch me." The doll Nadia was carrying got lost in the jostling crowd, and Nadia cried. She didn't understand the significance of what she had accomplished—and she didn't realize that her country's government would control her life completely from then on.

The next few years were difficult ones. Nadia wanted to go to movies and learn to drive like other teenagers. She began to clash with her coach and show up late for her practices. Finally, the Gymnastics Federation

decided to transfer her to a training center in the city of
Bucharest, where she would continue her gymnastics
with a different coach and also go to high school.

After her years of living under the strict control of
her previous coaches, Nadia wasn't sure what to do with
her new freedom. She went to movies and discos, slept
late, and ate all the foods she'd never been allowed to
eat. But she was unhappy. Her parents were getting
divorced, and she worried about them. She was growing
taller and going through puberty—and while this was
normal and healthy, she found it difficult to adjust to
her changing body.

But Nadia persevered. At sixteen, the Gymnastics
Federation allowed her to return to her former coaches,

and at eighteen, she was on her way to Moscow for the 1980 Summer Olympics, where she won another four medals.

To the Romanian government, Nadia was a valuable asset—they saw her as a symbol of their country's superiority. So, the following year, Nadia was sent on a tour in the United States, along with her coaches. The tour was called Nadia 81. At the end of the trip, Nadia's coaches decided not to return to Romania. At this time, citizens of Communist countries such as Romania were not allowed to leave. Those who left illegally or failed to return when they were supposed to were called defectors.

When Nadia returned to Romania without her coaches, her life changed dramatically. She was viewed with suspicion by her country's government, who were afraid that she would also defect. As a result, the government no longer allowed her to travel to competitions, which meant her career as an international gymnast was over. Over the next few years, Nadia struggled. It was hard to make a living and she was watched closely by the government and its secret police. She began to feel like a prisoner.

In 1989, Nadia decided she would defect as well. After months of planning, she made a daring escape, walking for hours through darkness and freezing temperatures to cross the border into Hungary. It was dangerous, and, if caught, she could have been shot—but Nadia made her way out of Romania and safely to the United States.

Nadia's incredible performance as a teenager helped inspire a new generation of young gymnasts. Today, she works directly with some of them. She runs a gymnastics school in Oklahoma, along with her husband—an American gymnast she first met at a competition when they were both teenagers.

Serena Williams

Unstoppable

Serena Williams has won four Olympic gold medals, three of them by playing doubles with her sister Venus. Their father was so determined that his daughters would be tennis champions that he wrote a detailed plan for their training—before they were even born!

Richard Williams was born into poverty and raised by his mother in the racially segregated community of Shreveport, Louisiana. When he met his future wife, Oracene Price, she was a single mom to three little girls, Yetunde, Lyndrea, and Isha. One day, Richard was watching television when he heard the announcer said that the winner of a tennis tournament, a young woman, had just earned $40,000! Richard vowed that he'd have two more daughters and get them started in tennis right away.

Richard didn't know anything about tennis, but he wasn't going to let that get in the way. He bought tennis books and videos, taught himself to play, and wrote a seventy-eight-page training plan to help his future daughters become tennis champions.

Venus was born in 1980, and just over a year later, on September 26, 1981, in Saginaw, Michigan, Oracene gave birth to another girl: Serena Jameka Williams. She was a still a baby when Richard and Oracene packed up their possessions and their five daughters, and they moved to Compton, California.

Serena's mom was a nurse. Her dad owned a security company, so his schedule was more flexible, and he was usually around during the day. The five sisters shared a bedroom with two bunk beds. The two older girls, Yetunde and Isha, slept on the top bunks, Lyn and Venus slept on the bottom bunks, and Serena—the baby of the family—climbed in with a different sister every night. "I felt like I belonged everywhere," she said.

Serena started going to the tennis court when she was still in her stroller, because her dad was already teaching the older girls to play. They practiced at public courts near where they lived, in Compton or nearby Lynwood; Richard and the five girls all squeezed into the family's van to get there. They had to take out the middle seat to make room for the shopping cart full of tennis balls and the brooms for sweeping the court. The courts were in rough shape, with cracked cement, weeds, litter, and broken glass, but Richard wrote inspiring words on big pieces of paper and hung them on the tennis court fence.

By the time Serena was five, she and her sisters were training for three or four hours every day. Serena grumbled occasionally, but her dad was good at making their practice time fun. He gave them plenty of play breaks to swing on the monkey bars and practice cartwheels—and if Serena needed an extra break, she'd hit her ball over the fence on purpose, so that she'd have to leave the court to find it!

Tennis made its way into their free time too. Serena, Venus, and Lyn invented a game they called Grand Slam, in which they hit a tennis ball back and forth with their hands. The court was a square on the sidewalk. They'd pretend they were at famous tennis competitions; to mimic the French Open, which is played on a clay court, they'd decorate the sidewalk square with dirt and for Wimbledon, they'd scatter a handful of grass.

Of course, not all their games were about tennis. They also liked to put on talent shows, and Lyn, Venus, and Serena would perform. Serena's performance was always the same: she sang Whitney Houston's "Greatest Love of All." The two oldest girls were the judges—but Serena couldn't stand to lose. "I'd kick and fuss until the judge made me the winner," she said.

Serena sometimes behaved badly, but she was the baby of the family and everyone always forgave her. Still, she once did something that she thought was so awful, she kept it a secret for years. All the girls had porcelain piggy banks, but when Serena accidentally broke hers, she was jealous that the other girls still had theirs. So she broke them all, one after another. It wasn't until at least a decade later that she finally confessed what she had done.

The older girls drifted away from tennis, so Venus and Serena played together. When they had practice matches, Serena often cheated. It was the only way she could beat her sister—and she hated losing! Venus never objected; she just kept on playing, each of them pushing the other and gaining strength and skill.

Their dad didn't want them to compete in tournaments too soon. He didn't want them to be under too much pressure, and he wanted to protect them from racism, as well. Tennis had a long history as a sport for wealthy white people, and there were still very few Black players. But when Venus was nine or ten, she wanted to compete. Finally, their dad agreed, on the condition that she had to beat him first. Richard was a strong player—but Venus won the match!

Soon, Venus was playing in national junior tennis tournaments—but Serena was still playing in local leagues against other little kids. One day, she saw an application for a tournament on the kitchen table and had an idea. The tournament was for ages ten and under. Venus was nine, and Serena was eight. Why shouldn't she go as well? Serena filled out an entry form, and when the day of the tournament came, she went along too. When Venus finished her match, their dad couldn't find his younger daughter anywhere. Finally, he found Serena playing a match on another court! Serena had expected to get in trouble, but when her dad saw her win, he was delighted. "I'm so proud of you," he said—and he added that since she had entered, she might as well keep playing.

That day, Serena won match after match. But suddenly, she realized something alarming: if she made it to the finals, she would have to compete against her own sister. "I knew I couldn't beat her," she said. "Venus was just too good, and I was just too little." She was right: Venus won their match. But her big sister found a way to cheer her up. She told Serena that she liked Serena's second place silver trophy better than her own golden one and traded trophies with her. Serena kept that gold trophy for her whole career. It was an important reminder that she and Venus might battle it out on the court, but they would always be sisters.

When Serena was nine, the family moved to Haines City, Florida, and a couple of years later, they moved again, this time to Pompano Beach. Moving was hard for Serena, and so was changing schools; she was scared other kids would pick on her. Her mom homeschooled her for a while, but Serena was in a slump, watching a lot of television and feeling a bit lost. For a while, she didn't even want to play tennis.

When Serena was ten and Venus was eleven, their dad decided that the girls shouldn't take part in any more national junior tournaments. He wanted them to enjoy being kids and focus on their education so that they wouldn't see tennis as their only option in life. He didn't like the extreme pressure that he saw many young players experiencing on the junior circuit—or the racist comments he had overheard people making about his daughters. He continued coaching the girls, and when Venus was fourteen, she convinced her father that she was ready to turn professional and compete in tournaments with adults. She entered a professional tournament in California, and Serena traveled with her. Venus played well and won more than $5,000, which seemed like a huge amount of money to Serena. She started begging her dad to let her enter a professional tournament too. He agreed, and at fourteen, Serena was on her way to Quebec City. But she was thrown off by the big crowd, the high expectations, and her own insecurities, and she played badly. "I wasn't ready," she admitted.

Serena kept training. She went to high school, and she gained confidence. She gained inches too, shooting up in height dramatically, which made her a more powerful player. The year she turned sixteen, she returned to professional tournaments—and this time, she wasn't just ready, she was unstoppable.

Two days after she turned nineteen, Serena had more than just a birthday to celebrate. She was in Australia, on the tennis court at the Sydney Olympics, with Venusand beside her, and they had just become the first sisters to win Olympic gold in doubles tennis. At the Beijing Olympics in 2008, they did it again—and at the 2012 Olympic Games in London, Serena won her first gold in singles competition. The next day, she was back on the court with Venus, and the sisters won yet another gold medal in doubles.

Serena went on to become the top ranked tennis player in the world. Before she retired in 2022, she won twenty-three Grand Slam singles titles (Grand Slam refers to the world's four most important tennis tournaments: the US Open, the French Open, Wimbledon, and the Australian Open)! Playing together, Serena and Venus also won fourteen major women's doubles titles. Serena is the world's highest-earning female athlete—and is considered the greatest woman tennis player of all time.

Ibtihaj Muhammad

Stronger than You Think

Fencer Ibtihaj Muhammad was not only the first Muslim American woman to win an Olympic medal—she was also the first woman to represent the United States at the Olympics while wearing a hijab. As a kid, Ibtihaj used to make hijabs for her Barbies. Today, there is a Barbie doll inspired by her!

Ibtihaj Muhammad's parents, Eugene and Denise, were both born and raised in Newark, New Jersey, and converted to Islam as young adults. They met at the mosque Eugene had founded and were married soon after. Ibtihaj was born December 4, 1985. She was their middle child, with two older siblings, Brandilyn and Qareeb, and two younger siblings, Asiya and Faizah. Ibtihaj's father was a police detective and her mother was a teacher.

When Ibtihaj was five years old the family moved to the nearby suburb of Maplewood. She had hoped there would be a backyard—but she didn't expect a huge swimming pool behind the house! Ibtihaj wanted to jump right in. Her father, whom she called Abu, had to remind her that she didn't know how to swim.

Ibtihaj quickly made friends with her new neighbor, Amy. The two girls spent lots of time together, riding their bikes on the driveway or playing with Barbies. One day Amy asked Ibtihaj why her mother wore a scarf over her hair. Ibtihaj explained that her mom wore a hijab because their family was Muslim—and was surprised to learn that Amy didn't know what this meant! Back in Newark, lots of the moms had worn a hijab, but this new community was much less diverse.

Ibtihaj's other best friend was her older brother Qareeb, whose high energy and wild ideas—like jumping off the top bunk bed—sometimes verged on hazardous. Ibtihaj didn't want to be left behind, even if their adventures ended in bumps, bruises, and tears. "I made it my life's mission to keep up with him," she said.

C'mon, don't be chicken!

Ibtihaj and her brothers and sisters were all expected to play sports. Her mom believed that sports would help them build confidence and stay out of trouble, and her father thought that participating in athletics would help make them successful in life. Ibtihaj tried tennis, T-ball, and track, but she wished she could play football like her brother Qareeb. She envied the way he fit in, wearing the same uniform as the other kids; because of her religion, she needed to cover her legs, so when she ran track, she wore long spandex leggings. The leggings were hot, and she hated that they made her look different from the other girls. All too often, Ibtihaj was the only Black girl, or the only Muslim—and dressing differently from others made her stand out even more.

When she started seventh grade, Ibtihaj began to wear hijab every day. She was proud of this sign of her maturity and her religious faith, but some of the other kids teased and bullied her. "I'd have to dodge insults being thrown at me walking down the hallway," she said. It didn't make sense to her. Why did anyone care if she wore a scarf to cover her hair? Qareeb told her she should stand up for herself—but Ibtihaj didn't want to speak up about what was happening. She just wanted to go to school and fit in with her friends. "They were free to be themselves and that's all I wanted too," she explained.

Ibtihaj loved everything else about school, so she tried to focus on that. At least her report cards were perfect! When she was eleven, her parents sent her to a summer program designed to help high-achieving Black and Latino students prepare for college. They learned essay writing and public speaking, how to apply to college, and how to manage their time. The teachers were supportive, and for once, Ibtihaj wasn't the only Black kid or the only Muslim. But she still had to get through one more year of middle school. Her new friend, Damaris, encouraged her to stay strong in the face of bullying, telling her, "You're stronger than you think."

That fall, Qareeb started attending Columbia High School, where Ibtihaj would go the following year. One day, when Ibtihaj and her mom picked him up, they saw students in the cafeteria wearing white pants, jackets, and masks who appeared to be sword-fighting. Qareeb explained that this was the fencing team. Ibtihaj wasn't very interested, but her mom was. Fencing was a sport in which Ibtihaj could wear the same uniform as the other kids while keeping her arms, legs, and hair covered as her religion required. The next thing she knew, her mom had contacted the team's coach and her dad was taking her for a private fencing lesson.

The lesson was in Coach Mustilli's garage. It had been turned into a gym, and there was a rack of swords and a long red rectangle painted on the floor. The coach explained that fencing, like chess, is a game of strategy—but it also requires the athlete to be strong, agile, and lightning fast. He grabbed a sword to demonstrate, showing Ibtihaj how fencers needed to keep their feet on the red rectangle, which he called the strip, and how they stepped and lunged at their opponent with the sword. Then it was time for her to try, and Coach Mustilli showed her how to stand, how to position her body, and how to hold her arms. But Ibtihaj's father, who had stayed to watch, felt uncomfortable—he didn't like the idea of his daughter taking private lessons in a stranger's garage. When they got home, he told her mom that Ibtihaj wouldn't be taking up fencing after all.

Ibtihaj wasn't particularly disappointed. As far as she was concerned, fencing was just one of many sports she had tried. But when she started high school and looked ahead to her future education, she began thinking about fencing again. Ibtihaj's parents had five kids to support, so she had to find a way to pay for college—and all the Ivy League schools had fencing teams. Could fencing help her earn a scholarship? She presented her plan to her parents, and they agreed that being part of a school fencing team was a good idea. Ibtihaj's new high school friends thought it sounded fun and agreed to join too— but when they all showed up for the first practice, they changed their minds. Most of the people in the room were white—and looked more nerdy than cool!

Ibtihaj was more concerned about getting into college than being popular. Besides, she'd heard that the fencing team included some of the smartest kids in the school. She might never fit in with the cool kids, but smart, nerdy kids could be her kind of crowd.

First, Ibtihaj learned that there were three different disciplines of fencing: épée, foil, and saber. She didn't know much about each discipline yet, but she decided to focus on épée and was given a light sword with a blunt tip. The best thing about fencing, she thought, was the uniform. Fencers wore special protective gear, known as fencing whites: long pants, long white socks, special fencing shoes, and on top, an underarm protector or half jacket, a chest protector, a jacket, and a glove. There was even a wire mesh mask that fit over her hijab. In their uniforms, the fencers were covered from head to toe—and for once, Ibtihaj looked just like everyone else.

Coach Mustilli demanded commitment from the team. They trained for three hours every day after school and on Saturday mornings, and soon Ibtihaj was going to competitions on Sundays as well. It was a lot of work, but she loved being part of the team. Even though she was the only Muslim, and one of just a few people of color, she'd finally found a place where she felt like she belonged.

ROAR!!!

Then, in her junior year, Coach Mustilli pulled her aside. He had overheard her letting out an aggressive roar as she lunged at her opponent—and that roar, he said, was the sound of a champion. Ibtihaj was pleased, but what her coach said next came as a shock. "I want you to come fence with the saber squad," he said. "Only a saber fencer roars like that."

Giving up épée was the last thing Ibtihaj wanted to do! She'd worked so hard to be good at it. Fencing saber would mean starting over; she'd have to use a different weapon and learn a new technique and a new set of rules. Besides, she liked her épée friends and wanted to keep practicing with them. "No, thanks," she said. But Coach Mustilli wouldn't take no for an answer. "I know a star when I see one, Ibti," he told her. "And you have the makings of a great saber fencer."

To Ibtihaj's surprise, he was right. From the first time she picked up the blade, she loved its lightness. It was made for speed! Épée was defensive—you had to try to stop your opponent from scoring points—but fencing saber meant taking the offensive. You could score by hitting your opponent with the side of the blade, not just the tip. It was faster, more aggressive— and, Ibtihaj thought, more exciting. Within a few weeks, she felt like she'd been fencing saber all along, and soon she was entering local competitions. Her father advised her to watch the winners and learn from them. Soon, Ibtihaj was the best fencer on her team, and it didn't take long before she was bringing home medals from local competitions.

That winter, Ibtihaj qualified for the Junior Olympics—the biggest national competition for young fencers—and she and her mom drove to Ohio for the event. Ibtihaj hoped to make it into the top sixteen—but instead, she was quickly eliminated. Crushed, she ran to her mother in tears.

But she didn't quit. She joined the Peter Westbrook Foundation, a fencing club in New York City that trained fencers of color. After finishing high school she attended Duke University—on a scholarship, just as she had planned—and in 2010, a few years after graduating from college, she became a member of the United States National Fencing Team. Over the next few years, Ibtihaj won five world championship medals—and in 2016, she was on her way to the Summer Olympics in Rio de

Janeiro. Ibtihaj won a bronze medal in the team saber event, becoming the first Muslim American woman to win a medal at the Olympics and the first America woman to represent her country while wearing a hijab.

She went on to become a public speaker, advocating for diversity and equality. *Time* magazine named her one of the world's "100 Most Influential People" and Mattel created a Barbie doll in her honor. "For little kids to walk up and down a toy aisle, to not only see a brown doll that's a fencer, but also have a doll who chooses to wear hijab, it's such a big moment," Ibtihaj said. She has written an award-winning picture book for kids too, *The Proudest Blue: A Story of Hijab and Family*, which draws on her own experiences wearing a hijab at school.

When the Olympics began in ancient Greece, there was only one event: a running race known as the stadion. It was named for the building the event took place in, and it gave us the word we use for sports arenas today, *stadium*. By the first modern Olympic Games in 1896, other track and field events as well as cycling, swimming, gymnastics, weightlifting, wrestling, fencing, shooting, and tennis had been added. Since then, many new sports have entered the Olympics (and a few, like croquet and tug-of-war, have later been removed).

At the 2020 Summer Games in Tokyo, karate, surfing, and skateboarding made their Olympic debut. The first-ever gold medal in women's street skateboarding was won by a thirteen-year-old, Momiji Nishiya, the youngest Japanese athlete to ever win a gold medal—and the third-youngest athlete ever to win a gold medal at a Summer Olympics! At the 2024 Summer Games in Paris, breakdancing will make history by becoming the first dance sport at the Olympic Games.

THREE

SWIMMING INTO SUMMER

THESE
SWIMMERS
★ ★ ★ grew up in ★ ★ ★
DIFFERENT COUNTRIES
AND AT
DIFFERENT TIMES,
BUT THEY ALL SHARED A LOVE
FOR THE WATER
—and a determination
TO BE THE BEST.

Gertrude Ederle

Queen of the Waves

Gertrude Ederle won three medals at the 1924 Olympic Games and became the first woman to swim across the English Channel. When she was a child, women were expected to wear long skirts and even stockings in the water!

Gertrude Ederle was born on October 23, 1906, in New York City. Her parents, Gertrude Anna and Henry Ederle were German immigrants, and Gertrude was the third of their six children. Henry owned a butcher shop on the West Side of Manhattan and the family lived in an apartment next door.

Around the corner from her dad's butcher shop was a blacksmith, who had a large water trough for horses to drink from. Three-year-old Gertrude used to run around the corner to the trough and jump in!

When Gertrude was five, she got sick with measles. Today, measles can be prevented by vaccination, but when Gertrude was young there was no vaccine, so measles was much more common. Gertrude survived the illness, but she did not escape the lifelong problems measles can cause. When she started school, one of her teachers told her parents that Gertrude was having trouble hearing in class. Her mom took her to see doctors and ear specialists, and they learned that the illness had caused permanent damage to Gertrude's hearing.

Gertrude was shy and a little self-conscious, but she liked being around other children. Playing sports, she discovered, was a great way to make friends. It helped that she was a naturally athletic kid. She played baseball and basketball. She also loved roller skating and used to zoom around her neighborhood on her skates at top speed.

When Gertrude was seven, her family took a trip to Europe to visit Henry's mother in Germany. In 1914, traveling to Europe meant a week-long trip across the ocean on a big steam-powered boat. During their time in Germany, Gertrude and her sisters Meg and Helen had an adventure that could easily have ended in disaster: They found a wobbly wooden plank that led to the town's dam and decided to walk along it. All three girls fell into the water, causing a panic among the locals who thought that the American children might drown before they could be fished out.

This near disaster didn't scare Gertrude away from the water—but it did make her want to learn to swim.

The following year, Gertrude's family bought a summer cottage in Highlands, New Jersey. The Shrewsbury River ran right by their bungalow—it was just off their porch! Gertrude desperately wanted to get in the water, but the river had a strong current and moved swiftly. One day, she persuaded her father to lower her in to the water, with a sturdy rope tied around her waist for safety. Gertrude loved being in the water, just as she had ever since she was a toddler playing in the horses' water trough. Her very first stroke was the dog paddle. Being in the river was so much fun that she wanted to do it again and again. She wanted to learn how to swim fast!

Gertrude had seen local men swimming in the river and noticed how they used their arms to propel themselves. She wanted to do that too. So she practiced and practiced, and within a few weeks she could swim. The other swimmers sometimes laughed at her wild strokes, but she didn't care.

The next few summers were all about swimming. Gertrude put on her swimsuit after breakfast and didn't take it off until bedtime. She loved swimming and she wanted to go fast! One year, at an end-of-summer carnival, she raced against other local kids. She beat them all easily, and one of the people watching suggested that she join the newly founded Women's Swimming Association of New York (WSA). Gertrude liked the idea—so she, Meg, and Helen all joined.

The WSA was trying to create more opportunities for women swimmers. They also wanted better swimsuits! When Gertrude was born, women had to swim in suits made of heavy fabric—often with long skirts and even stockings—but by the time she was in her teens, women swimmers were working to change this tradition and beginning to wear more practical clothing to swim.

The indoor pool used by the WSA was only thirty feet long, less than one-fifth of the size of an Olympic pool—but membership to the WSA was cheap and it gave Gertrude and her sisters a place to swim year-round. It also gave them access to training. The club's volunteer swimming coach, Louis de Breda Handley, had been on the 1904 Olympic water polo team! On Gertrude's first day at the pool, he asked her to swim a length so he could see how she swam. Gertrude dove in and swam, not even stopping to breathe—and as she reached the end of the pool, she overheard the club's diving coach telling him that Gertrude would never be a good swimmer. Gertrude was furious—and even more determined to succeed.

Handley was working to develop a new stroke—one that would be faster and more efficient than the Australian crawl that was popular at the time. Instead of having his swimmers turn on their sides and do a scissor kick when they needed to breathe, he taught them to maintain their body position and merely turn their heads to take a breath. This stroke became known as the American crawl; Gertrude was one of its early adopters. She practiced in the pool all winter and in the river during the summer. During her first year with the WSA, when Gertrude was twelve, she swam in her first formal race in a municipal pool, and a year later, she went to Detroit to race in a team relay. She and her teammates didn't just win—they set a world record!

At this time, competitive sports were dominated by men. Women were not encouraged to be involved in athletics at all—it was seen as unladylike. Gertrude's parents expected her to keep up with her responsibilities at home and didn't make allowances for her swim schedule. She was sometimes late for practices because she was busy cleaning, ironing, or doing the dishes.

When Gertrude was sixteen, her sister Meg tried to convince Gertrude to join her for a long-distance swim: a 3.5-mile race from Manhattan Beach to Brighton Beach. Gertrude had swum only short races and was reluctant to enter. In the end, it was her dad who persuaded her. He wanted her to keep busy—and out of trouble—while he and his wife took a trip to Germany, so he told Gertrude if she joined all Meg's races that summer, he would agree to let her get a fashionable bob haircut! So Meg filled out their entry forms, and the two sisters swam daily, practicing ever-increasing distances in the Shrewsbury River.

The race was a big deal; newspaper headlines proclaimed that the best women swimmers ever would be facing off against each other, including the American and British all-around champions. When the race began, Gertrude got off to a quick start, and maintained her lead for the whole race, doggedly swimming through rain and rough water. Her time shattered previous records, and it would be decades before anyone else matched it.

That summer, Gertrude broke one record after another. Another swimmer joked that she must have propellers on her feet! The following summer, she was even faster—and breaking her own records. Gertrude left school after tenth grade so that she could focus all her energy and time on swimming. She traveled around the US, as well as to Canada, Bermuda, and even Europe, taking part in competitions along with other WSA swimmers. She was still shy, and her deafness made conversation difficult sometimes; she was often happiest when she could bury herself in a mystery novel. But her success was fueling a new wave of interest in women's swimming.

Gertrude was seventeen when she boarded a ship to France for the 1924 Olympics. It was only the second time America had sent a women's swim team to the Olympics and Gertrude was excited to be part of it. Unfortunately, the US officials were worried that the Paris night life would be a bad influence on the young women, so they booked them rooms in a hotel outside the city. This meant that she and her teammates spent up to five hours a day on the bus, traveling back and forth between their hotel and the pool where they practiced. On top of that, Gertrude was having trouble with a muscle injury. Unsurprisingly, she didn't swim as well as she had hoped. Still, she won a gold medal and two bronze medals! When she returned to New York, she and the other swimmers were paraded down Fifth Avenue and tens of thousands of people took to the streets to cheer for them.

By age eighteen, Gertrude was a professional swimmer, which allowed her to be financially independent, and by nineteen, she had set twenty-nine world records. But her greatest victory was yet to come.

For long distance swimmers, one of the ultimate tests of endurance is to swim the English Channel: a cold, rough, twenty-one-mile stretch between England and France. Since 1875, only five men had done it. Gertrude wanted to be the first woman.

In her first attempt, when she was eighteen, she failed. Her heavy bathing suit had a high neck that rubbed and chafed her skin, and the suit kept filling up with water as she swam, weighing her down. In the boat that was keeping pace and looking after her, people became concerned that she was swallowing too much salt water. To break the world record as an unassisted solo swimmer, Gertrude was not allowed to touch the boat or any other person, but her coach, thinking she was drowning, tried to rescue her. Gertrude insisted that she was fine—she had just been resting—but because another person touched her, she was automatically disqualified.

Gertrude fired that coach and hired another, and a year later, she was ready to try again. This time, she designed her own suit—a lighter, tighter two-piece swimsuit that she made by cutting a one-piece suit in half! She even designed her own goggles. She wanted to look decent, she said, in case they had to drag her out of the water. At the time, a two-piece swimsuit was considered quite bold.

On August 6, 1926, she entered the water in France, facing six-foot waves and freezing water. Her body coated in a thick layer of grease to protect her from the cold, she set off. By the time she arrived at the English coast, after fourteen and a half hours of nonstop swimming, a huge crowd was waiting to welcome her. Not only was she the first woman to swim across the English Channel, but she had also beaten the fastest previous man's time by two hours. Her record stood until 1950.

"When somebody tells me I cannot do something, that's when I do it," Gertrude said. "People said women couldn't swim the Channel, but I proved they could."

Michael Phelps

The Boy Who Couldn't Sit Still

Sometimes known as the Flying Fish, Michael Phelps is the most successful Olympian ever: he has won a record-breaking twenty-eight Olympic medals! At his first swimming lesson, however, he didn't even want to get his face wet.

Michael Phelps was born on June 30, 1985, in Baltimore and raised in the nearby suburb of Towson. His mom, Deborah Sue (or Debbie), was a home economics teacher and his dad, Michael Fred Phelps, was a Maryland state trooper. Michael was the baby of the family. His older sisters, Hilary and Whitney, were seven and five years old when he came along.

Right from the start, Michael was a high-energy kid who got into everything. "Whatever it was, if it was breakable, I usually found it," he said. "I simply could never sit still." Even at the dinner table, he had to be busy. He would play with the saltshaker or twirl a steak knife between his fingers. He'd play with his food too, mixing everything on his plate together and adding sugar and mayonnaise as if he was making a casserole. Sometimes he'd pour milk on top and eat the resulting concoction. "It drove my mom crazy," he said.

To make matters worse, he never seemed to listen to warnings. One night at a Mexican restaurant, his parents told him to be careful of the hot sauce. Michael couldn't resist the challenge—and besides, he thought, it looked just like ketchup. He dumped a huge spoonful of hot sauce on a tortilla chip and popped it in his mouth. Instantly, his eyes began streaming with tears as he waved his arms frantically. Way too hot!

When Michael was seven, he came home one day to find his sisters in tears. His mom explained to Michael that she and his dad were separating.

Around this time, Michael learned to swim. Both of his older sisters were swimmers, so Michael had grown up around the pool and was excited to finally get in the water. But the pool wasn't anything like he had expected, and at first, he hated it. "We're talking screaming, kicking, fit-throwing, goggle-tossing hate," he said. Most of all, he didn't want to get his face wet. He made excuse after excuse: he was too cold, he had to go to the bathroom . . .

But his swimming teacher persisted, and Michael gradually became more comfortable in the water. Once he learned to swim, he loved it. "I felt so free," he said. He swam every day and stayed in the water for as long as possible.

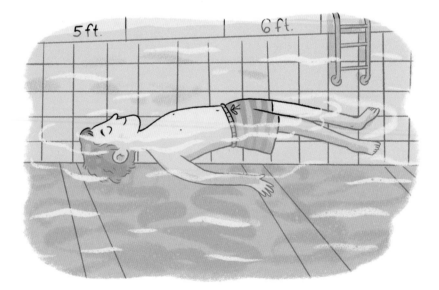

Michael was a busy kid. In addition to swimming, he played lacrosse and baseball, and he enjoyed being around his sisters and his friends. But he was also a sensitive kid, and when his parents' separation became a divorce, it hit him hard. Often, he felt abandoned by his father.

School was tough too. The other kids made fun of the way Michael spoke, teasing him about having a lisp. Michael was self-conscious about his appearance as well; he thought his ears were much too big. He often wore a hat to make them look smaller, but other kids had figured out that teasing Michael about his ears was an easy way to get a reaction. Sometimes they would grab his hat and make comments about Spock, the Vulcan character from *Star Trek* with notably pointy ears.

One of Michael's teachers complained to his mom that he couldn't concentrate on anything. But most people were more patient with him. His third-grade teacher told Michael it was healthy to have an "active personality."

When Michael was in sixth grade, some of his school troubles started to make more sense after he was diagnosed with attention deficit hyperactivity disorder (ADHD). He began taking medication and found that it helped him focus. He didn't take it on weekends, though, and at swim meets his behavior was sometimes a little wild. "I was either running off to the side to play with the other kids, banging my kickboard against the pool deck or sneaking to the front of the line to jump into someone else's race," he said.

But despite his trouble focusing, Michael's talent as a swimmer was undeniable. By the time he was ten, he held the national record for his age group in the 100-meter butterfly. At eleven he began training even more seriously. His new coach was named Bob Bowman. Bob was strict, and with him around, Michael couldn't get away with anything—the coach seemed to have eyes in the back of his head! If Michael splashed a teammate or hid someone's cap, Bob would notice. One of the swimmers stuck a sign on Bob's door that said "Beware of Bob."

During his years at Dumbarton Middle School, Michael continued to have challenges in the classroom. Writing was difficult for him. Sometimes he didn't remember to hand in assignments, and sometimes he just didn't bother doing them. His quick temper got him in trouble too; once, another kid kept flicking at Michael's ears during a volleyball game, and Michael punched him. Michael was suspended, and his mom talked to him about learning better ways of resolving conflicts.

But he had a lot of fun with his friends at the pool. One of their games was speaking a made-up language called Bong. To speak Bong, you added -*ong* to the consonant sounds in a word and said the name of the vowels. The word *hot*, for example, would become *hong-oh-tong*. The best part about speaking Bong was that their coach couldn't understand what they were saying.

Or so they thought. One day, Bob handed Michael a note with realistic goals to aim for at his next swim meets. To Michael's shock, the note was written in Bong! Bob hadn't been fooled by the made-up language at all.

In 1999, Michael started ninth grade at Towson High School. He really wanted to play football, and maybe golf as well, but finally realized that swimming wouldn't leave him enough time for other sports. It was a sacrifice that he and his coach thought was worth making; Michael was winning races and breaking records, and Bob was starting to think that the Olympics were within reach.

Sure enough, at age fifteen, Michael was on his way to Sydney for the 2000 Summer Olympics. He was the youngest swimmer on a US team since 1932. On the flight to Australia, one of the flight attendants invited Michael and the two other teenagers on the team to come up to the cockpit. They looked out the window and saw Sydney Harbor and the Opera House down below!

Michael enjoyed his first Olympics. He didn't win any medals, but he swam well, clocking some of his best times ever. When he returned home, his mom arranged for a limousine to pick him up from the airport, and some of Michael's friends came to meet him there. They took the limo to the 7-Eleven for celebratory Slurpees. When Michael arrived back at his high school, expecting to head to his usual classes, he was caught by surprise: the school had secretly planned a party. There were television cameras and banners, and people wearing buttons and T-shirts that said FLY MICHAEL FLY. Some of the other students even wanted his autograph!

In keeping with a US swim team tradition, Michael got a tattoo of the Olympic rings on his hip. He was already looking forward to the next Olympics, four years away—but no one could have predicted quite how successful he would be at them.

In 2004, Michael won eight medals—six of them gold—at the Summer Olympics in Athens. In Beijing in 2008, he won another eight gold medals—one in every event he entered, seven of them in record-breaking time. No athlete had ever won so many medals at a single Olympics! At the London Games in 2012 and then Rio de Janeiro in 2016, Michael continued to break records and collect medals—in fact, at four Olympic Games in a row, he won more medals than any other athlete. He is considered to be the greatest swimmer of all time.

Ellie Simmonds

Wanting to Win

British swimmer Ellie Simmonds has won eight Paralympic medals, five of them gold—and she won the first two when she was just thirteen years old. As a small child, she loved sports—from riding horses to ballet—but thanks to a backyard pool and a fierce determination to win, it was swimming that made her a star.

Ellie's full name is Eleanor May Simmonds, and she was born in England on November 11, 1994. She is the youngest of five siblings, but by the time she was born, the three oldest—Steven, Pauline, and Georgina—had already grown up and moved out. Ellie's sister Katie is the closest in age; she is five years older than Ellie, and the two girls grew up together near Birmingham in the West Midlands. Both Ellie and Katie have achondroplasia, a genetic condition that affects bone growth and causes people to be very short, which is called dwarfism. Many people with dwarfism also describe themselves as dwarfs or Little People.

Ellie was an energetic kid who liked to be outdoors and needed to be busy. "From the moment I could talk I'd be asking my mum what we'd be doing that day—I didn't do sitting quietly on my own very well!" Luckily, there was usually plenty to do: her grandparents all lived nearby, and Ellie saw them every day. She also had many aunts, uncles, and cousins in town—and of course, her older siblings. Ellie's grandmother taught her to bake, and Ellie loved making cakes, muffins, and scones. She also enjoyed going for long walks and bike rides, and having picnics in the park with her parents and siblings. And then there was swimming! Ellie's family had a backyard pool and she loved spending time in the water. She started taking swimming lessons shortly before she turned five.

Around the same time, Ellie started school. "I found it really hard to keep up," she said. "Nothing had time to sink in before we moved on to the next thing." Then Ellie's family moved to a new house and Ellie changed schools. At first she was sad to leave her friends, but she made new friends easily, and she was much happier at Aldridge School. Ellie especially enjoyed phys ed and art. "I was always happier when I was doing something active," she said. Luckily, she was nearly always doing something active! She took dancing classes and ballet, she went to Girl Guides (the UK equivalent of Girl Scouts) meetings, and she loved riding horses and spending time at the stables.

She also swam. Her first swim at a local swimming club didn't go well: even in the shallow end, Ellie couldn't touch the bottom of the pool, and the instructor was so worried about her drowning that he insisted on carrying her for the whole lesson! But the Boldmere Swimming Club proved to be a much better fit, and Ellie joined along with her sister Katie. When she was seven, Ellie was invited to join the squad—a team of young swimmers ready to move on from swimming lessons to twice-weekly training sessions. After a few months, her coach suggested she needed to swim three times a week—and over the next two years, that became four times, and then five. Ellie enjoyed training and made close friends with the other swimmers. "For me it was all about having fun . . . there was always lots of laughing and messing around!"

The other swimmers in the squad were all able-bodied and of average height, so Ellie had to work hard to keep up. Most of the time, though, dwarfism didn't feel like an obstacle for Ellie. "I'm just small. I can do everything everyone else can do," she said. Having short arms and legs did make some things more difficult—like reaching shelves in shops, having to get clothes altered to fit, and finding shoes she liked in her size. But when it came to swimming, being short was a significant disadvantage. Ellie was always competing against athletes who were much taller than her, so she rarely won and didn't realize how talented she was.

When she was nine, the Summer Olympic and Paralympic Games took place in Athens, and Ellie watched the swimmers on television. "Watching Nyree

Lewis get her medal in the 100 meter backstroke inspired me to want to go to a Paralympics," she said.

A year later, Ellie took part in her first British Junior Para-Swimming Championships. She competed in the under-14 category and won every race she entered. "Winning felt amazing," she said. "Suddenly my competitive nature kicked in and I just wanted to win all the time." Before competitions, Ellie started looking at the previous finish times of her rivals and highlighting the names of those whose times were close to her own—those were the people she needed to beat. "My parents used to call it my hit list!" she said.

In Paralympic events, athletes compete against others with the same disability classification. These classifications range from level 1, for the athletes with the most severe disabilities, to level 10, for the athletes with very minor disabilities. Ellie was classified as S6—or swimmer level 6—because of her height. Athletes with an S6 classification can have many different types of disability—one might have dwarfism like Ellie, another might be an amputee, and another might have cerebral palsy, like Ellie's hero, Nyree Lewis (now Nyree Kindred). Regardless of their differences, the race is fair because S6 swimmers all have a similar amount of power in the water.

When Ellie was eleven, she was swimming fast enough to qualify to compete internationally. The IPC Swimming World Championship, a biennial event now known as the World Para Swimming Championships, was coming up in South Africa, but Ellie worried she might be too young to be chosen to take part. Athletes had to be at least twelve years old to compete internationally, and Ellie's twelfth birthday was just two weeks before the competition! She tried not to get her hopes up—and was thrilled when she was selected for the team.

Ellie had a wonderful time in South Africa. She loved everything about the experience: the hot weather, training in an outdoor pool, and seeing lizards and monkeys along the road. She didn't win any medals, but she swam her best-ever times in all her races.

Ellie's family knew that she needed specialized coaching and the opportunity to train with other para swimmers, and that wasn't available in Birmingham. So she and her mom moved to the town of Swansea in South Wales, where she could work with coach Billy Pye. Her dad stayed behind to run the family business. Ellie had to change schools, and she missed her friends, her dad, and the rest of her family. Every weekend, Ellie and her mom drove three hours to stay one night at home and then drove three hours back to Swansea. "I'd sleep the entire ride just to make it go faster," Ellie said.

Being apart was a sacrifice for everyone—but it paid off. When Ellie was thirteen, she made the British Paralympic team and was on her way to swim in Beijing, China, where she became the second-youngest

British Paralympian to win a medal. And she didn't just win one; Ellie came home with two gold medals and a new world record. She even beat Nyree Lewis, who won the silver.

Ellie found all the attention a little overwhelming—especially when she returned to Swansea and discovered that her school was holding a special event to celebrate her success. "I just wanted to go back to normal, because I think of school as a normal place," she explained.

Afterward, Ellie was nominated for the 2008 BBC Young Sports Personality of the Year. This is an award given in Britain each year to the young athlete who has made the most significant contribution to sports. Ellie was thrilled to attend a big event with lots of famous athletes. She didn't expect to win, so she didn't practice a speech—but then her name was called as the winner!

A year later, at fourteen, Ellie became the youngest person ever to receive an MBE, or Member of the Order of the British Empire. This is a very important honor in the United Kingdom and the award was presented by Queen Elizabeth. Ellie wore high heels for the first time ever, but at the last minute she changed into flat shoes because she was worried that she might trip. "I thought the worst thing I could do was end up flat on my face in front of the Queen," she said. She put the heels back on when she posed for photographs afterward, though.

Over the next few years, Ellie trained hard, swimming at least eighteen hours a week while attending high school. When she was seventeen, she competed in the 2012 Summer Paralympic Games in London. Because the event was in Ellie's own country, she received a lot of media attention. There was even a giant picture of her on the side of a building facing the Olympic Park! The excitement of the crowds at the sold-out events made Ellie even more determined, and she swam her way to two more gold medals, as well as a silver and a bronze—and she broke two more world records.

Four years later, Ellie won a gold and a bronze at the 2016 Paralympics in Rio de Janeiro, breaking yet another world record—and in 2021, she traveled to Tokyo for her fourth Paralympics, where she was given the honor of being a flag bearer at the opening ceremony. Although Ellie didn't win a medal in Tokyo, finishing in fourth place, she thoroughly enjoyed herself. "I've had a wonderful competition and I've loved every minute of it," she said.

Ellie retired from competitive swimming after Tokyo, but one thing hasn't changed: she still likes to be busy. She is an advocate for youth athletics and a strong supporter of the Dwarf Sports Association. She has taken part in several British TV shows—from a comedy baking show to a dance competition—and written a series of children's books called Ellie's Magical Bakery. She is also an activist who works hard to promote paralympic sport and to educate people about dwarfism. "I wouldn't change myself," Ellie says. "I love who I am and I am glad that I have dwarfism because I think my body is strong and beautiful."

Yusra Mardini

A Team That Defies Borders

When Yusra Mardini watched the Olympics on television, she vowed to become an Olympic swimmer herself—but when her country was torn apart by war, that journey became more difficult than she could ever have imagined.

Yusra Mardini was born in Syria on March 5, 1998. She lived with her mother, Mirwat, her father, Ezzat, and her older sister, Sara, in Daraya—a suburb of Syria's capital city, Damascus.

Yusra's father was a swimming coach at the Tishreen Sports Center in Damascus. Determined that his daughters would be champion swimmers, he signed them up for training at the sports center. Yusra was only four, and she wasn't very interested—the water was cold and she preferred to sit outside, but saying no to her father wasn't an option. She was a Mardini, he said, and Mardinis were swimmers.

When she was six, Yusra and her father watched the 2004 Olympic Games on television. The men's

100-meter butterfly race was about to begin, and Yusra's dad pointed at one of the swimmers. "Watch lane four," he said, and Yusra gazed at the screen as Michael Phelps powered through the water, overtaking the swimmer in front of him to claim the gold medal. Yusra made a silent vow: She would follow Phelps to the top. One day, she too would swim at the Olympics.

A few weeks later, Yusra started school. She also joined the Damascus youth swimming team alongside her sister, Sara. Every day after school, they went to the pool for two hours of training. Her father was very strict; in the car driving to and from the pool, swimming was the only subject they were allowed to talk about.

When Yusra was nine, her sister joined the national team. It was wonderful news for Sara, but Yusra was going through a difficult time: First, she was accidentally hit by a piece of weight-training equipment and needed stitches. Then she got a painful ear infection—and finally, she learned she needed glasses. She got an itchy red rash on her neck that worsened whenever she was stressed—and that year, it seemed like she was stressed a lot.

Then Yusra learned something surprising: her mother was pregnant. At first, Yusra was anxious. She was the baby of the family, and she wasn't sure she wanted that to change. But when her little sister was born, Yusra was thrilled. They named the baby Shahed, which meant *honey*.

When Yusra was twelve, she joined the Syrian national swim team. She knew she was one step closer to her dream. But by the spring of 2011, when she turned thirteen, anti-government protests were spreading across the Arab world. On television, Yusra and Sara watched the news about the uprisings in Tunisia, Egypt, and Libya. Their father said nothing like that would ever happen in Syria, but one day on the school bus, Yusra's friend whispered news to her: in the nearby city of Daraa, not far from where Yusra's mother taught water aerobics, some kids had been arrested for writing anti-government graffiti on a wall.

Over the next few days and weeks, Yusra heard more rumors. She learned that people were protesting the arrest of the kids in Daraa. Protests were happening in other cities too—even in Damascus—and there had been violence at some of the protests.

One day, Yusra's mom came home from work, shaking. There had been huge explosions, and the army had evacuated people from the area. Yusra and Sara were no longer allowed out in the evenings. Sometimes they heard gunfire or explosions. Soldiers walked the streets, stopping cars, questioning people, checking their identification. One day, the soldiers even boarded the school bus and searched under the seats! Yusra and Sara couldn't imagine what they were looking for on a bus full of kids.

A few days before Yusra was about to fly to Russia for her first international competition, her family was driving home from a visit to Yusra's grandmother when they found their route blocked by army tanks. A soldier pointed a gun at their car and yelled at them to leave. When Yusra's father hesitated, the soldier shot at the ground in front of them! Yusra was terrified. The tires screeched as Yusra's dad slammed the car into reverse. When they were finally able to return to their neighborhood, electrical poles and wires lay across the street, shops windows were smashed, and there was broken glass everywhere. Another soldier yelled at them to leave the area. Shaken and scared, they drove back to Yusra's grandmother's house. Yusra stayed there until it was time for her to board her flight to Russia.

Yusra swam well at her competition, helping her relay team win two bronze medals. But when she returned to Syria, her family was still staying with her grandmother and there were army tanks on the streets of Daraya. Yusra never saw her house again. It wasn't even safe to go back for photographs and other precious possessions; all Yusra had was the bag of clothes she'd taken to Russia.

Yusra's father was offered a job coaching swimming in Jordan, and he decided to take it. The money he earned would allow Yusra, Sara, Shahed, and their mother to rent an apartment in Damascus. Sara stopped swimming because of an old shoulder injury, but Yusra kept training. She even set a new Syrian record for the 400-meter freestyle.

Swimming was the one normal thing in Yusra's life—until the day a bomb hit the athletes' hotel right beside the stadium where Yusra swam. She had been nearby when the bomb fell, and she was badly shaken. She decided she wasn't going to swim anymore. It was too dangerous—she could have been killed. The rebellion had become a civil war, with government forces fighting the rebels. Despite the violence around her, Yusra tried to go on with her life. She finished ninth grade, spent time with Sara and her friends, and took Shahed out for booza—a chewy, stretchy ice cream served with chopped pistachios.

Some of Sara's friends had already left Syria, making their way to Europe, and Sara began talking about leaving too. Yusra wondered what she would do if Sara left. Would she go with her? She couldn't imagine leaving her country.

Finally, she decided to return to swimming. She knew it wasn't safe—but she wasn't safe anywhere. She began training for two hours a day in the pool, followed by an hour in the gym.

One night when Yusra was seventeen, she was swimming laps when there was a thunderous crash. The coach yelled at everyone to get out of the water. As Yusra ran for the exit, she looked up and saw a hole in the roof of the building. Then she looked down—and there, lying at the bottom of the pool, was a meter-long grenade. If the bomb had landed on either side of the pool and hit the tiles, it would have exploded.

Yusra's mother picked her up from the pool that day and begged her to stop swimming. But Yusra couldn't give it up. "Swimming is my life," she told her mother as they drove home. "I'll have to go to Europe."

For Yusra and Sara, getting out of Syria was the easiest part—in 2015, it was possible to fly to Turkey without a visa—but traveling to Europe from Turkey was difficult and often dangerous. Many refugees entered Europe by taking boats from Turkey to Greece. These boats were operated by smugglers who charged desperate passengers a lot of money for the crossing.

Yusra and Sara's boat was a cheap inflatable dinghy loaded with twenty people—three times the number it was designed to carry. The smugglers abandoned the passengers, leaving them to drive the boat themselves, and after fifteen minutes in the open water of the Aegean Sea, the engine failed and the boat began to fill with water. The passengers threw everything they could over the sides—their bags, even their shoes—but the boat was still too heavy. So Sara, Yusra, and two men jumped overboard. They took turns swimming and holding the boat's rope, guiding the boat and preventing it from being swamped.

One of the passengers was a six-year-old boy, and even from the icy water, Yusra did her best to cheer him up. "The little kid kept looking at me, scared," she said, "so I was doing all these funny faces." But inside, she feared they would all drown. "We were pulling and swimming for their lives."

For more than three hours, they swam and hoped—until, finally, the boat's engine started again. That night, they arrived on the shore of the Greek island of Lesbos. Yusra was cold and aching. She had lost her shoes and her glasses. But she was alive.

This long journey was just beginning. Next, the refugees took a ferry to Athens, on the Greek mainland, and began walking north, hiding in cornfields at dusk, terrified that they would be caught by police and sent back. Finally, nearly a month after they left Syria, they arrived in Berlin, Germany, where they asked for

asylum as refugees. One of the first things Yusra
wanted to know was whether there was somewhere she
could swim!

The Olympics seemed like an impossible dream
now—Yusra no longer had a country to swim for. But
something unexpected happened. The International
Olympic Committee was planning a new team for the
2016 Olympics in Rio de Janeiro—the Refugee Olympic
Team—and Yusra was one of the athletes being
considered! At first, she wasn't sure how she felt about
this. She wanted to go to the Olympics because she was
the best in her country, not because she was a refugee.
But she realized it was an opportunity to spread an

important message: that no one chooses to be a refugee and that people who have had to flee their countries can still achieve great things.

Yusra swam in Rio, competing under the Olympic flag of the Refugee Olympic Team. In 2017, she was made an ambassador for the United Nations High Commissioner for Refugees. And in 2021, she carried the flag of the Refugee Olympic Team in Tokyo, where she competed in her second Olympic Games. Speaking about her team, she said, "We chose to keep our dreams alive. We carried them with us across oceans and deserts and cities. We brought them together to form a team greater than ourselves, one that defies borders and limits, a team that belongs to everyone."

The Olympics and the Paralympics are elite competitions for the world's strongest, fastest, and most skilled athletes—but the Special Olympics is based on the idea that sports are for everyone.

The roots of the Special Olympics go back to 1960, when a woman named Eunice Kennedy Shriver became concerned about the lack of opportunities for kids with intellectual disabilities. She decided to host a summer camp at her Maryland farm and invited local schools to send young campers with disabilities and teenage volunteers to support them. Over the next few years, Camp Shriver grew, and similar camps and programs started up across the country.

This movement led to today's Special Olympics: the world's largest sports organization for people with intellectual disabilities. With an emphasis on inclusion, it runs more than 100,000 events every year, ranging from local competitions to huge international ones—like the 2023 Special Olympics World Summer Games in Berlin.

FOUR

SPEAKING OUT

★ ★ ★ **THESE** ★ ★ ★

OLYMPIANS

didn't just break records

OR WIN MEDALS—

THEY ALSO USED THEIR

VOICES

TO STAND UP FOR

JUSTICE AND
EQUALITY

and to make our world

A BETTER PLACE.

Tommie Smith

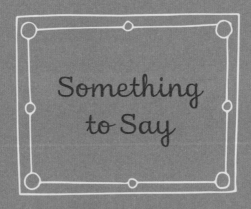

Something
to Say

I n 1968, twenty-four-year-old Tommie Smith
stood atop the podium, a gold medal around
his neck. He had just run 200 meters in world-
record time—but it was what he did next that
made Olympic history.

Tommie Smith was born on June 6, 1944, in Clarksville, Texas. His parents, James Richard and Dora, lived nearby in the tiny community of Acworth, and Tommie was the seventh of their twelve children.

Tommie's parents were sharecroppers: they farmed land owned by white people, picking and chopping cotton. Like most sharecroppers, they worked very hard and remained poor. Because of the way the sharecropping system was designed, many farmers such as the Smiths ended up owing more to the landowner than they were able to repay. Tommie's family's house was small and the roof leaked; when it rained, they put buckets on the floor to catch the drips. On winter evenings, they huddled in front of the wood stove.

Most of the time, Tommie was outdoors. His earliest memory was of going fishing with his dad and older siblings. On the way to the pond, they had to cut through a marshy area where Tommie spotted tiny fish. He wondered why they didn't catch those fish instead—but when he tried to grab one, he discovered they were way too fast!

The kids called their mother Mulla. She was hardworking, quiet, and strict about the kids being neat and clean. Tommie was very close to her and loved to hear her laugh. He looked up to his dad too, admiring his strength and stamina. Like the rest of his family, Tommie worked hard, helping in the fields or digging water holes for the hogs—but there was time to play too, and plenty of brothers and sisters to play with.

When it was time for Tommie to start school, he walked to the schoolhouse with his sisters Sally and Hattie. It was a two- or three-mile walk each way. The schoolhouse had a single big classroom, and the students all learned together, with kids of different ages sharing one teacher. In Texas at this time, Black children and white children went to different schools. This was the law, part of a system of segregation that kept Black people and white people apart and discriminated against Black people. Tommie didn't know where the school for the white kids was, but he knew they didn't have to walk miles like he did; they rode in a wagon. He knew that white people owned the fields his family worked in and the house they lived in. And he saw the way white people talked to his father. "I was quite young and I didn't know exactly what I was seeing," Tommie said, "but I knew somehow that what I saw wasn't the way it was supposed to be."

When Tommie was six, his family moved from Texas to California—a two-day ride on a crowded bus. The driver wouldn't stop often for bathroom breaks, so the kids had to pee in jars! For the next two years, they lived in a labor camp in the valley south of Fresno and worked in the fields—picking corn, sugar cane, grapes, and lettuce, as well as picking and chopping cotton like they had in Texas. This was how the family paid off what they owed for the bus ride.

At first, the kids all worked too—but one day, a man followed them onto the bus that took them to the fields each morning. His name was Mr. Smith and he was the principal of Stratford Elementary school. All the kids had to get off the bus and go to school, he told them. In California, this was the law.

At Tommie's new school, the Black kids and white kids were all in the same classroom, but Tommie couldn't help noticing that they were not treated the same way by the teachers. The white kids always got to go first—whether they were asking questions, getting balls to play with, or going to recess. Some of the white kids bullied the Black kids. Once, when Tommie was six, a boy knocked his ice cream from his hand and told him that Black kids didn't eat ice cream.

Finally, the Smith family's debt was paid and they left the labor camp, moving to a house outside Stratford, California. Their new house was built on stilts, so you could see all the way underneath it, and there was no glass in the windows, so it was always drafty.

Moving meant that Tommie started at a new school—and he accidentally repeated second grade! Back at his old school, there had been a number two above his classroom the door, so when Tommie arrived at his new school, Central Union Elementary, he headed straight to the classroom marked with a number two. "That's how I ended up in the second grade two years in a row," he said.

Tommie's athletic skill was becoming obvious: at his new school, all the kids wanted him on their kickball team. It was important to Tommie to do well in his classes—and to look good. By fourth grade, he took great pride in washing and ironing his own clothes. "I hated to bend my knees because I might break the crease in the pants," he said.

One day, Mr. Focht, who coached the track team, saw Tommie's sister Sally run. She beat all the other students easily, so he told her to get her brother out of the fourth-grade classroom and race him. Sally was in seventh grade, and Tommie had never beaten her before—but that day, he did. "That was the first big race in my life," he said.

Mr. Focht helped Tommie's dad get a job as a janitor at the school, and the family moved to a new house, one with a lawn, flushing toilets instead of an outhouse, and a television. It was just a short walk to school, and for Tommie, it was the first place that felt like home.

By eighth grade Tommie was six foot three and very strong. He enjoyed sports, and he was good at all of them: baseball, flag football, basketball. But the older he grew, the more he noticed the racism that surrounded him. "Being white was desirable, being black was not. That is what society taught us at the time," he said. Every day, Tommie saw the differences in how the white students and the Black students were treated, and it made him feel bad about himself. He didn't even like to ask questions in class, because he was ashamed of the way he spoke.

When he started high school at Lemoore High, Tommie felt overwhelmed at first—the school was huge! But playing football and basketball soon helped him make friends, and he joined the school track team too. Tommie's parents were too busy to attend his track meets, but his sister Sally always took an interest. In his junior year, he set national records as a runner—and in his senior year, he broke them himself.

College coaches took notice, and many of them offered him scholarships. Tommie decided to go San Jose State University. As a student, he spent a lot of time in the library. He read about the history of Black people in America and began to understand more about the role that history had played in creating the society he lived in.

As a student, Tommie tied the world record for the 200-meter race. It was 1965—the height of the civil rights movement for Black rights in America—and the day after his race, Tommie took part in a civil rights march, walking for twelve hours. It was the first time he had joined a group to stand up for human rights.

Three years later, Tommie qualified for the US Olympic team—but he wasn't sure if he would go to Mexico for the 1968 Summer Games. In the year leading up the Olympics, a group of athletes and activists had come together to organize a boycott; they said they wouldn't take part in the Olympics unless steps were taken toward ending racial discrimination. Called the Olympic Project for Human Rights (OPHR), the group had been started by a professor at Tommie's university—Dr. Harry Edwards—and Tommie and his San Jose State teammate John Carlos were the first two athletes to join. At first OPHR was focused on racism in the United States, but as the Olympics drew closer, the group's aims became global. In the end, one of their demands was met—South Africa and Rhodesia, countries with white minority governments and racist laws (for example, South Africa, whose population was mostly Black, allowed only white athletes to compete in the Olympics!) were uninvited—and the OPHR athletes decided to attend the Games.

Tommie ran the 200-meter sprint in less than 20 seconds, breaking the world record and winning a gold medal. John Carlos won the bronze. The two athletes decided to use their moment on the podium—those few seconds when the eyes of the world would be on them—to make a statement. They each raised a black-gloved fist and stood silently, their heads lowered. Afterward, Tommie explained: "My raised right hand stood for power in black America. Carlos's left hand stood for the unity of black America." Tommie also wore a black scarf, as a symbol of Black pride, and they both wore black socks with no shoes, as a symbol of Black poverty in the United States. The silver medalist, a white Australian runner named Peter Norman, stood in solidarity with them, an OPHR pin on his jacket.

The silent protest made headlines around the world. Some people supported the athletes, but others said that the Olympics was the wrong place to make a political statement. Tommie disagreed. "If you are one of the world's greatest in a particular field . . . you have an avenue and you have a responsibility to use it, especially if you have something to say about society and how people are treated," he said.

US Olympic officials, under pressure from the International Olympic Committee expelled Tommie Smith and John Carlos from the Games and banned them from the Olympic Village. Back at home, Tommie faced criticism by the media and received death threats from strangers. Even his family was harassed. Tommie was one of the fastest men in the world, and still in his early twenties—but he was banned from any future Olympic competition. It was a difficult time, but Tommie stood his ground. "I had no regrets, I have no regrets, I will never have any regrets. We were there to stand up for human rights and to stand up for black Americans," he said.

After the Olympics, Tommie played football, earned a master's degree in social change, and became a university instructor and track coach. He published his memoir, which he titled *Silent Gesture*. And in 2008, after sprinter Usain Bolt set three world records at the Beijing Summer Games, Tommie presented him with one of his shoes from the 1968 Olympics—a birthday gift from one Olympian to another.

Megan Rapinoe

> ## Everybody's Responsibility

As a captain of the United States soccer team, Megan Rapinoe twice helped lead the way to Olympic gold. As an athlete, she uses her voice to speak up for justice—but when she was a kid, she sometimes got in trouble for talking too much.

Megan Rapinoe and her twin sister, Rachael, were born on July 5, 1985, in Redding, California. Rachael was older by eleven minutes. They were born into a big family: two older half-siblings, Michael and Jenny; an aunt, CeCé, who was fifteen and more like a sister than an aunt; and a five-year-old brother named Brian. When the twins were babies, their mom's sister Melanie and her daughter also moved in!

Megan's mom, Denise, was used to big families. She was the second of eight kids, and because Denise's parents were both alcoholics, she'd played a big role in taking care of her younger siblings. When she met Jim Rapinoe, she had her hands full with her first kids, Michael and Jenny, as well as her nine-year-old sister,

CeCé. Jim had worked as a fisherman, a car salesman, and a crane operator. After Denise and Jim married, Brian was born—and then five years later, the twins arrived.

Megan and Rachael were athletic kids who, from the time they could walk, liked to chase soccer balls around the big oak tree in their yard. When they saw Brian do a trick, they would instantly copy it. They needed to see a trick only once to be able to do it themselves. Their sister, Jenny, remembered thinking, "My sisters are going to get gold medals one day."

When Brian was ten years old, he started playing soccer on a local team. Megan and Rachael watched his games avidly. "Every time they did something cool, we ran up and down the sidelines trying to imitate them," Megan said. There wasn't a girls' soccer team for Megan and Rachael to join, but they had caught Brian's coach's eye and the next year, when they were six years old, the girls were invited to join the under-8 boys' team.

Megan was thrilled. "Every Saturday morning before practice, I got up super early to put on my uniform," she said. She loved her uniform—a white T-shirt with black piping around the neck. She loved the clicking sound her cleats made on the floor. In fact, she loved everything about soccer. She and Rachael were unbeatable, with soccer skills far ahead of the boys on their team. "They're going to be in the World Cup one day," their coach told their parents.

The fact that Megan and Rachael were twins was an advantage. Every day, they practiced together after school, riding their bikes to the soccer field behind Cow Creek Community Church and playing until the sun went down. Perfectly matched in both skill and ambition, they pushed each other hard, both of them wanting the other to be their absolute best. "When one of us messed up or gave less than 100 percent, the other would swoop down on her and scream insults while the rest of the team looked on in horror," Megan said. "To us, yelling at top volume at each other was completely normal."

Megan had tantrums as a little kid—and if she was angry or upset, she hated to be comforted. She would feel overwhelmed by her rage and she was too embarrassed to let anyone see her feeling out of control. Luckily, her parents were relaxed and accepting; the kids were who they were, Denise said, and as Megan grew older, she learned to manage her emotions.

Their mom worked at night, so their dad did the dinner-and-bedtime routine. Once a week, he'd announce that it was time for "rake-out!" This meant it was leftovers night, and time to clean out the fridge and eat whatever they found there. It was the kids' least favorite meal. "We hate rake-out!" the kids would yell. At dinner, they all sat at the table together and talked about their days. Mornings were when they talked to their mom—or Mammers, as they called her. She'd be there, in her pajamas, when they woke up and they'd sit on her lap and talk. "Even in high school we'd still sit on her lap," Megan said.

Denise's job was at a local steakhouse called Jack's Grill. She'd worked there since the twins were toddlers. Megan loved it: it was cozy and the staff all knew her. After school, she and Rachael would go there to sit on the bar stools and eat crackers. "We thought it was the most glamorous place in the world," Megan said.

When Megan was ten, something terrible happened: Brian, her kind, funny, charming brother, was arrested for possession of drugs and sent to juvenile detention. It was the beginning of many difficult years as Brian's life was devastated by drug addiction. Their parents tried everything they could to help, but addiction is very powerful and Brian's drug use continued. "My sister and I didn't understand much of it, at first," Megan remembered. "We were too young." Besides, she and Rachael were so busy with school, friends, and soccer. But as they got older, Brian's problems became impossible to ignore. When Megan was thirteen and Brian was eighteen, he was sent to prison for stealing a car. He would spend most of the next two decades in and out of prison. At first, Megan felt sorry for him, but soon she felt angry as well. He was hurting their whole family so much. As she got older, she realized that the problem was bigger than Brian and his choices—and that sending people who were addicted to drugs to prison did nothing to help them recover.

Soon after Brian's arrest, Megan's dad decided to start a girls' soccer team for his daughters to play on. They'd been playing on boy's teams for four years! He would be the team's coach. But while both he and their mom were always supportive and encouraging, they didn't push the girls. The drive to play always came from Megan and Rachael themselves. From age six onward, Megan said, they were obsessed with soccer and fanatically self-motivated.

By age eleven, Megan was up before the sun rose every weekend so that she, Rachael, and their parents could drive the two and a half hours to Sacramento for games and practice at eight in the morning. Having kids who were serious about soccer was a big commitment for the whole family, but as Megan got older and had soccer games farther away, even out of state, she enjoyed the family road trips. "My mom would look up awesome places to eat on the road," Megan recalled. Her one objection was the family's minivan, which she and Rachael considered very uncool.

When it came to soccer, Megan was serious—but off the field, she was a playful kid who liked making people laugh. "I ran around making fart noises," she said. "I was a goofball." But when she started sixth grade, all the other kids seemed to have grown up over the summer. "All of a sudden, the girls didn't run around with the boys anymore." The girls sat around and talked and, somehow, playing ball at lunch was now something only the boys did. Megan had always been confident and popular, but now she felt very uncomfortable: "I didn't know where I fit in or how to behave," she said.

Rachael wasn't having the same struggles: she was enjoying her social life, and she seemed to know what to wear and how to act. Megan wasn't interested in clothes at all, so she just wore whatever Rachael told her to. Megan wasn't interested in boys either. Other girls would talk about which boys they thought were cute, and Megan felt mystified and bewildered. For the next few years, she tagged along behind Rachael, letting her sister make all the social decisions.

She coped with her confusion by focusing harder than ever on soccer, developing her skills and her style as a player. In 1999, when the FIFA Women's World Cup was held in the US, Megan stuck posters of the US team on her bedroom wall—and two years later, she got an exciting phone call. The US under-17 women's national team was inviting her to play an international youth game in France! She could hardly believe it. A huge package came in the mail, full of T-shirts, sweatshirts, shin pads, and cleats branded with the US team logo—and a few weeks later, Megan was pulling on a USA shirt and playing soccer in France.

Playing at this level required sacrifices for the whole family. For Megan and Rachael, there was little time for high school dances or parties; as teenagers, the people they spent the most time with were their parents, traveling to practices, training camps, and tournaments. "At an age when most of our friends were off partying, we were with our parents in the minivan," Megan said. Luckily, the girls had good relationships with their parents and enjoyed their time together. When Megan and Rachael were high school sophomores, their family grew unexpectedly: Brian and his girlfriend had a baby they couldn't look after themselves, so Megan's parents decided that little Austin would join their family.

When it was time to attend college, Megan and Rachael assumed they would go off to school together. Their mom insisted that they visit every school that was offering them scholarships. They chose the University of Portland and planned to start together in the fall of 2004—but then Megan got another startling phone call. The US women's national team was inviting her to play in the under-19 world championship in Thailand! She would have to start college a semester late. Rachael went off to attend her first semester at the University of Portland without her sister, while Megan began training with the national team, flying to Thailand to compete.

During Megan's first semester of college, she realized she was gay. Coming out made her much happier. Finally, she felt free to dress and act how she wanted—to truly be herself. Eight years later, Megan was getting ready for the Olympic Games in London when she decided to come out more publicly. Her friends and family all knew she was gay, but the larger world did not. Her team's silver medal win in the 2011 FIFA World Cup had rocketed Megan into the public eye, and she felt a responsibility to use her voice to create change. "The more people who come out, the more we break down the stereotypes of what it is to be gay," she said. Over the next couple of years, as the fight for marriage equality headed to the Supreme Court, Megan felt proud to have spoken up.

Megan helped lead the United States to a gold medal win at the 2012 Olympics, famously becoming the first-ever athlete to score directly from a corner kick at the Olympic Games. And she continued to use her platform to stand up for social justice. In 2016, during a US national team game in Chicago, she knelt during the national anthem. It was a gesture of solidarity with football quarterback Colin Kaepernick, who had been using this same action to protest racism and to stand up for Black lives in America. "I feel like it's actually everybody's responsibility to use whatever platform they have to do good in the world and to try to make our society better," she said.

Simone Biles

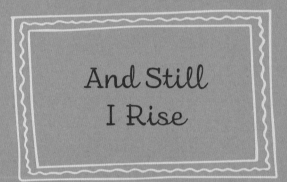

And Still
I Rise

American gymnast Simone Biles is often called the GOAT: the greatest of all time. She has won seven Olympic medals and twenty-five world championship medals—more than any other gymnast. Her physical strength was evident from the start: as a little kid, she used to do pull-ups on her older brothers' outstretched arms!

Simone Arianne Biles was born in Columbus, Ohio, on March 14, 1997. She has an older sister and brother, Ashley and Tevin, and a little sister named Adria. Unfortunately, their birth mother, Shanon Biles, had problems with drugs and alcohol and wasn't able to care for the kids well, so when Simone was three, she and her siblings were taken into foster care. Their foster parents were kind and had a dog the kids could play with. There was a trampoline in the foster family's yard, too—but Simone wasn't allowed on it. After a few months, Simone's grandfather—Shanon's father, Ronald Biles—came to pick them up. The kids were going to stay with him and his wife, Nellie Cayetano Biles, while Shanon received treatment.

Simone's grandparents lived in a suburb near Houston, Texas, with their teenage sons. Her grandfather had grown up in the housing projects of Cleveland. He was one of nine kids and had joined the air force after high school. Nellie was from Belize and had come to the United States at eighteen to study nursing. When Simone was young, she called them Hamma and Hampaw because she couldn't say Grandma and Grandpa.

Simone thought her grandparents' house was beautiful. Her grandparents bought Barbies and clothes for her, and the room she shared with her sisters had shelves filled with new books. But best of all was what she spotted outside: a trampoline! And this time, she got to use it. "For what seemed like hours, I bounced and twirled and flipped and somersaulted," she said.

Simone and her baby sister, Adria, were happy with their grandparents, but Ashley and Tevin missed their mother. When it became clear that Shanon would not be able to raise her children, Ashley and Tevin moved in with their Aunt Harriet in Cleveland so they could stay closer to her. Meanwhile, Simone's grandparents began the lengthy process to adopt Simone and Adria.

Simone's grandpa had been the one who chose her name; as a teenager, he'd been a big fan of Nina Simone. "I've always loved knowing that he was the one who named me," Simone said. It made her feel like he'd been watching over her from the very beginning. When Simone was six, she and Adria put on their fanciest dresses—blue for Simone and pink for Adria—and went to the courthouse with their grandparents to finalize the adoption. That very night, Simone began calling her grandparents Mom and Dad.

Simone was a fearless kid with boundless energy, and she was always climbing and jumping, running and roughhousing. Her big brothers Ron and Adam used to bounce her on the trampoline to see how high she could fly and how many flips she could do in the air. Her mom sometimes worried she'd get hurt, but Simone loved it. She might be small but she was strong too; she used to climb up her brothers' bodies to sit on their shoulders or ask them to hold their arms out for her to do pull-ups!

One rainy day, Adam, who was now teaching at Simone's day care, decided to take the all the kids to the nearby gym for a field trip. It was the first time Simone had seen gymnastics equipment—beams and bars and vaults—and she couldn't wait to try it out. She came home with a letter inviting her to enroll in classes at Bannon's Gymnastix, and her mom signed her up that same week. Simone was thrilled. Her coach, Aimee Boorman, later described her first impression of Simone: a tiny muscular girl who couldn't sit still.

Simone's sister Adria tried out gymnastics too, but she didn't love it like Simone did and decided to join Girl Scouts instead. The rest of the time, the two girls were inseparable. They played hopscotch, jump rope, and soccer. They rode their bikes, making zooming noises and pretending they were riding motorbikes, or they drove their toy cars around, pretending to be cops and giving each other tickets. One of their favorite games was one they called "Trying Not to Laugh": one girl would take a big mouthful of water and the other had thirty seconds to make her laugh and spew water everywhere.

One day, Simone and Adria were riding their bikes on their street when they spotted something on the ground: three small blue eggs. One was crushed and had yellow fluid trickling out, but the other two were whole. "Let's save them so the babies can hatch," Simone said. Back at home, they gently put the eggs in a plastic container and filled it with warm water. But the next afternoon, when they checked on the eggs, the water was cloudy and yellow—the eggs were leaking! Simone and Adria were horrified: had they killed the baby birds? But their neighbor Marissa started to laugh. "Those aren't bird eggs!" she said. Simone and Adria had been trying to hatch paintballs.

One day, playing in the backyard, Simone spotted a rock on the ground and tossed it over the fence. To her surprise, there was a splash. "Is there a pool over there?" Adria asked, picking up another rock and throwing it. *Splash!* The girls thought this was hilarious. Throwing rocks over the fence into the neighbor's pool became their new favorite game—until they decided to climb the fence so they could see their rocks landing in the water. Their neighbor caught them in the act and told their mom. Until then, he'd thought his dog was responsible for the rocks in his pool!

At the gym, Simone was mastering new skills at a speed that stunned her coaches. She was learning four main types of apparatus: floor, beam, vault, and her least favorite, the bars. "I'm just not good at bars," she told her coach. She was short, with small hands, and the bars were so high! They scared her. But she practiced until she was dreaming about her routines when she fell asleep at night.

By the time Simone was in sixth grade, she was
competing—and winning—against much older
gymnasts. She was starting to dream big, fantasizing
about making the national team and going to the
Olympics. There was a big competition coming up—the
level nine Western Championships—and to qualify for
it, she knew she needed to score high at a regional
championship. Simone was determined to do it: her dad
had told her that if she qualified, they could get a dog.
She and Adria had been begging for a puppy for years.

When the big day came, Simone performed all her
routines beautifully, taking first place on floor and
second place all-around. When her score flashed up on
the scoreboard, she heard Adria, who was watching
from the stands, start screaming, "We're getting a dog!"

A few months later, a German shepherd puppy joined the family. Simone named her Maggie Elena.

At home and at the gym, Simone was happy. At school, however, she was not. Because she needed to spend thirty hours a week training, she'd switched to a private middle school close to her gym for seventh and eighth grade. She missed her old friends—and her new teacher didn't even bother to learn her name. All year long, he called her Somalia because there was a map of Somalia on the wall behind her. On top of that, she found it hard to focus and was easily distracted. She was finally diagnosed with ADHD and began taking medication, which helped a lot.

In the gym, however, Simone had no trouble

concentrating: "I could be laser focused," she said. Still, the next couple of years presented many challenges. A bad fall on the bars shook her confidence, and she was heartbroken when she wasn't chosen for the 2011 USA women's junior team. Perhaps hardest of all, she had to make a difficult decision: should she go to the public high school where she'd be reunited with her oldest friends, or should she be homeschooled so that she could pursue a career in elite gymnastics? She wanted both. Part of her dreamed about being an ordinary teenager—but in the end, after a lot of tears and a few temper tantrums, she chose gymnastics.

Five years later, Simone won her first Olympic gold medal at the 2016 Summer Olympics in Rio de Janeiro.

By the end of that year's Olympic Games she had collected five medals, four of them gold—and by 2022, she had won an incredible twenty-five medals at World Championship events, more than any other gymnast in history.

But Simone's contributions to the world of gymnastics go beyond the athletic and artistic. When she and many other young American gymnasts experienced abuse by their team's doctor, she spoke up about her experiences and demanded that those who failed to protect the young athletes be held accountable. In 2021, Simone got a tattoo of Maya Angelou's words on her collarbone: "and still I rise." It is a line from a poem about Black pride, surviving and overcoming oppression and abuse, and the strength of the human spirit.

In a sport in which athletes are too often pushed to take risks, it takes courage to choose self-care over medals, but Simone did so at the Tokyo Olympics. When she lost her sense of body awareness as she tumbled through the air—a dangerous occurrence that gymnasts refer to as the twisties—she withdrew from the event, helping start an important conversation about mental health.

In 2022, she was awarded the Presidential Medal of Freedom by President Joe Biden. At twenty-five years of age, Simone Biles was the youngest person to ever receive this honor.

Naomi Osaka

A Call to Action

Naomi Osaka is a four-time Grand Slam singles champion and the first Asian tennis player to be ranked number one in the world. As a kid, her main goal was to beat her older sister on the court—but as an adult, her goal is to change the world.

Naomi Osaka was born on October 16, 1997, in
Chūō-ku, Osaka, in Japan. Her mother, Tamaki Osaka,
is from Japan, and her father, Leonard François, is from
Haiti. When Leonard was in college, he visited
Hokkaido, where he met and started dating Tamaki.

Tamaki was afraid that her father wouldn't approve
of her new boyfriend, so she kept their relationship a
secret. When her father began talking about arranging
a marriage for her, Tamaki told him that she already
had a partner. Tamaki's father held racist views and
didn't want Tamaki to marry a Black man. So Tamaki
left Hokkaido, moving to Osaka with Leonard. Their
first child, Mari, was born in 1996 and Naomi in 1997.
Tamaki and Leonard gave their daughters Tamaki's last
name: Osaka.

When the girls were toddlers, Leonard was watching television when he saw Venus and Serena Williams playing at the French Open. When he heard that their father had taught the two sisters to play tennis, he was inspired. Leonard decided to follow Richard Williams's training plan. "The blueprint was already there," he said. "I just had to follow it."

When Naomi was three years old, her family moved from Japan to the United States. For the next five years, they lived on Long Island with Leonard's parents. For Naomi, it was a chance to be surrounded by her father's Haitian culture. Her grandparents spoke Haitian Creole and cooked spicy Haitian stews. But she was still deeply connected to Japan, too, and her mom spoke to her and Mari in Japanese.

In those early years on the tennis court, Naomi and Mari played together. Mari was older but Naomi was more driven to win. "I don't remember liking to hit the ball," she said. "The main thing was that I wanted to beat my sister. For her, it wasn't a competition, but for me, every day was a competition. Every day I'd say, 'I'm going to beat you tomorrow.'"

Life in the United States wasn't easy. Leonard was completely focused on coaching the girls in tennis, and Tamaki worked hard to support the family. Tamaki also did all the housework and cooking. She made the girls Japanese-style bento lunchboxes every day, with rice balls called *onigiri*. Mari and Naomi weren't allowed to eat processed food or candy, but a few times a year, as a treat, they would have homemade cake and ice cream.

Even with Tamaki working multiple jobs, money was tight. There were a lot of expenses: tennis equipment, court fees, and travel, as well as the regular living costs for a family of four. Once, when the girls begged their mom to take them ice-skating, Tamaki poured oil on the floor to make it slippery—they could skate at home, she said.

The family also faced racism in the United States—and particularly within the tennis world. "Tennis is still a sport for the white community," Naomi's mother said, explaining that some people didn't like seeing Black and Asian people training hard. Sometimes, when the girls were playing on public tennis courts with their father, other players even called the police, reporting that an unlicensed coach was teaching.

In 2006, Naomi and her family moved to southern Florida, where there were more opportunities for young tennis players. The girls were homeschooled, focusing on their studies in the evenings. All day long, they practiced tennis. "I honestly wasn't really good as a kid," Naomi said. "We were literally on the court every day for at least eight hours. So I was just, like, tired."

Two years later, when Naomi was eleven, her mom decided it was time for her and Mari to meet their Japanese grandparents. For Naomi, a highlight of the visit was seeing the fashions in Tokyo's Harajuku district. "Living in Florida, everyone would just wear jeans and T-shirts, and in Japan people were wearing tutus," she said. "It was so expressive."

Back at home, Naomi's life continued to revolve around tennis. Mari was her best friend, and on long car rides to tournaments, the two of them drew creative outfits and fashions in their notebooks. Naomi was shy, and she didn't have much time to socialize with other kids anyway. "She used to spend all her free time at home either playing video games or chatting with her sister," her mother said.

Many young tennis players in Florida competed in tournaments on the junior circuit, but because Leonard wanted Naomi to follow the path trodden by Serena and Venus Williams, Naomi skipped most of these tournaments and moved directly into the women's circuit, playing against adults at fourteen. She and Mari were becoming strong players, but they were not yet well-known.

That changed overnight when Naomi was sixteen and she defeated the former US Open champion in a match. "Sixteen-year-olds aren't supposed to hit serves that clock in at 120 mph, but that's precisely what Osaka did," one reporter wrote. Two years later, Naomi was ranked in the world's top fifty women tennis players. And two years after that, at age twenty, Naomi defeated her idol, Serena Williams, to win the US Open—and 3.8 million dollars! She was the first Asian tennis player to be ranked number one in the world.

Growing up without much money, Naomi had
always hoped that her tennis could help her family
financially. She knew how hard her mom worked. "She
would work overtime. She would sleep in her car
sometimes. For me, that was the whole point of playing
tennis. It was honestly either become a champion or
probably be broke." Naomi's dad was the parent
everyone saw, because he had been on the court
coaching her as kid, but it was her mom's efforts behind
the scenes that made it possible. "My mum sacrificed a
lot," Naomi said. "We would go to tournaments, and she
would stay at home and work because someone had to
pay for the flights and stuff. I'm very grateful for
everything she's done."

Naomi's parents also helped her make important decisions about her tennis career—like which country she would represent in international competitions like the Olympics. As a citizen of both Japan and the United States, she could choose to compete for either country. When she was young, her parents had decided they wanted her to represent Japan, and when she was old enough to understand, she agreed. "I don't necessarily feel like I'm American," she said. "As long as I can remember, people have struggled to define me. I've never really fit into one description—but people are so fast to give me a label. *Is she Japanese? American? Haitian? Black? Asian?* Well, I'm all of these things together at the same time."

In May 2020, a Black man named George Floyd was killed by a Minneapolis police officer. "I felt a call to action," Naomi said. She flew to Minneapolis and joined peaceful demonstrations on the streets. Like many people, she donated money, signed petitions, and went to protests—but it didn't feel like enough. "I kept asking myself what can I do to make this world a better place for my children? I decided it was time to speak up about systemic racism and police brutality."

In August, after another Black man was killed by the police, Naomi withdrew from an upcoming tournament. "Before I am an athlete, I am a black woman," she wrote on social media. "And as a black woman I feel as though there are much more important matters at hand that need immediate attention, rather than watching me play tennis."

A few weeks later, Naomi competed at the US Open. This was in the early months of the COVID-19 pandemic, and every time Naomi stepped on to the court, she wore a face mask bearing the name of a Black American killed by police violence: Breonna Taylor, Elijah McClain, Ahmaud Arbery, Trayvon Martin, George Floyd, Philando Castile, and Tamir Rice. She wanted to honor their names, and she wanted to get people talking about racism and police brutality.

The Olympics that year were to be held in Tokyo, Japan—something that had special meaning for Naomi, who was representing the country of her birth. At the opening ceremony for the Tokyo Games, she was given the honor of lighting the Olympic cauldron—the first tennis player ever to do so. She said it was the greatest athletic achievement and honor of her life.

Naomi didn't win a medal at the Tokyo Olympics—but her presence at the games had meaning beyond the tennis court. "I am proud . . . of the small part I have played in changing perceptions and opinions," she said. "I love the thought of a biracial girl in a classroom in Japan glowing with pride when I win a Grand Slam. I really hope that the playground is a friendlier place for her now that she can point to a role model and be proud of who she is. And dream big."

Many people experience challenges related to their mental health, but in our society, we don't always do a good job of talking about these difficulties. Some Olympians are working to change that.

Michael Phelps struggled with depression, anxiety, and thoughts about suicide for many years. For a long time, he kept this secret, partially because as an Olympic champion, he felt so much pressure to look strong. Since then, he has begun to use his story to raise awareness and encourage others to seek the support they need. So have Naomi Osaka and Simone Biles! They both began speaking up publicly about this topic after they withdrew from competitions to focus on their mental health.

These three athletes want young people to know that they aren't alone. "It's OK to not be OK," Simone says, and Michael agrees. "Struggles and stress are a part of life and the human experience," he says. "It's okay to ask for help."

Further Reading

Bibliography

There are many wonderful books about Olympians, including auto-biographies (books written by the person about their own life) and biographies (books about noteworthy people written by someone else). This is a list of some of the main sources used by the author in researching and writing this book.

PART 1

Jesse Owens

Baker, William J. *Jesse Owens: An American Life*. Chicago: University of Illinois Press, 2006.

Schaap, Jeremy. *Triumph: The Untold Story of Jesse Owens and Hitler's Olympics*. Boston: Houghton Mifflin, 2007.

Wilma Rudolph

Smith, Maureen A. *Wilma Rudolph: A Biography*. Westport, CT: Greenwood Press, 2006.

Usain Bolt

Bolt, Usain, and Matt Allen. *Faster than Lighting: My Autobiography*. London: HarperSport, 2013.

Tatyana McFadden

Bonhôte, Ian, and Peter Ettedgui, dir. *Rising Phoenix*. HTYT Films and Passion Pictures, 2020. Netflix.

McFadden, Tatyana, and Tom Walker. *Tatyana McFadden: Ya Sama! Moments from My Life.* N.p.: Inspired Edge, 2016.

PART 2

Dick Fosbury

Welch, Bob, and Dick Fosbury. *The Wizard of Foz: Dick Fosbury's One-Man High-Jump Revolution.* New York: Skyhorse Publishing, 2018.

Nadia Comăneci

Comăneci, Nadia. *Letters to a Young Gymnast.* New York: Basic Books, 2004.

Serena Williams

Williams, Richard, and Bart Davis. *Black and White: The Way I See It.* New York: Atria Books, 2014.

Williams, Serena, and Daniel Paisner. *On the Line.* New York: Grand Central Publishing, 2009.

Ibtihaj Muhammad

Muhammad, Ibtihaj. *Proud: My Fight for an Unlikely American Dream.* New York: Hachette Books, 2018.

PART 3

Gertrude Ederle

Dahlberg, Tim, Mary Ederle Ward, and Brenda Greene. *America's Girl: The Incredible Story of How Swimmer Gertrude Ederle Changed the Nation.* New York: St. Martin's Press, 2009.

Michael Phelps

Phelps, Michael, and Brian Cazeneuve. *Michael Phelps: Beneath the Surface.* Champaign, IL: Sports Publishing, 2012.

Ellie Simmonds

Ewing, Sarah. "Interview: Ellie Simmonds: My Family Values." *Guardian*, September 5, 2014. https://www.theguardian.com /lifeandstyle/2014/sep/05/ellie-simmonds-my-family-values.

Simmonds, Ellie. *Swimming the Dream.* London: Harper Collins, 2012.

Yusra Mardini

Mardini, Yusra, and Josie Le Blond. *Butterfly: From Refugee to Olympian—My Story of Rescue, Hope, and Triumph.* New York: St. Martin's Press, 2018.

Wilder, Charly. "She Swam to Escape Syria. Now She'll Swim in Rio." *New York Times*, August 1, 2016. https://www.nytimes.com /2016/08/02/sports/olympics/a-swimmer-goes-from-syria -to-rio-from-refugee-to-olympian.html.

PART 4

Tommie Smith

Bradley, Adam. "The Timeless Appeal of Tommie Smith, Who Knew a Podium Could Be a Site of Protest." *New York Times Style Magazine*, August 6, 2021. https://www.nytimes.com/2021/08/06 /t-magazine/the-timeless-appeal-of-tommie-smith.html.

Smith, Tommie, and David Steele. *Silent Gesture: The Autobiography of Tommie Smith*. Philadelphia: Temple University Press, 2007.

Megan Rapinoe

Rapinoe, Megan, and Emma Brockes. *One Life*. New York: Penguin Press, 2020.

Simone Biles

Biles, Simone, and Michelle Burford. *Courage to Soar: A Body in Motion, a Life in Balance*. Grand Rapids, MI: Zondervan, 2016.

Macur, Juliet. "Simone Biles and the Weight of Perfection." *New York Times*, July 24, 2021. https://www.nytimes.com/2021/07/24 /sports/olympics/simone-biles-gymnastics.html.

Naomi Osaka

Bergeron, Elena. "How Putting on a Mask Raised Naomi Osaka's Voice." *New York Times*, updated September 4, 2021. https://www .nytimes.com/2020/12/16/sports/tennis/naomi-osaka-protests -open.html.

Haskell, Rob. "Leading by Example: How Naomi Osaka Became the People's Champion." *Vogue*, December 11, 2020. https://www .vogue.com/article/naomi-osaka-cover-january-2021.

Larmer, Brook. "Naomi Osaka's Breakthrough Game." *New York Times Magazine*, August 23, 2018. https://www.nytimes.com /2018/08/23/magazine/naomi-osakas-breakthrough-game.html.

Naomi Osaka. Lauren Cioffi, Katy Murakami, and Sally Rosen, producers. Film 45 and Uninterrupted, 2021. Netflix.

Index

N

O

P

156; Rio de Janeiro (2016), 156–57; Tokyo (2020), 66, 157

Phelps, Deborah Sue (Debbie), 136, 137, 139

Phelps, Hilary, 136

Phelps, Michael, 11, 135–45, 159–60, 223

Phelps, Michael Fred, 136, 137, 139

Phelps, Whitney, 136

police brutality, 220–21

polio, 32

Price, Isha, 96, 97

Price, Lyndrea, 96, 97, 99, 100

Price, Yetunde, 96, 97

Pye, Billy, 153

R

racism, 16–29, 32, 34, 101, 104, 177, 178, 181, 216–17, 220–21. *See also* civil rights; segregation

Rapinoe, Austin, 197

Rapinoe, Brian, 188, 189–90, 192–93

Rapinoe, Denise, 188, 191–92

Rapinoe, Jim, 188–89, 191, 193

Rapinoe, Megan, 10, 187–99

Rapinoe, Rachael, 188, 189–90, 192, 193, 194, 195, 196, 197

Refugee Olympic Team, 169–70

Riley, Charles, 22–25

Rudolph, Blanche, 31, 32, 33

Rudolph, Ed, 31

Rudolph, Wilma, 10–11, 30–41

They're Little Kids with Big Dreams . . . and Big Problems!